CHRISTIANITY IS CREDIBLE

Christianity is Credible

LOUIS-MARIE DE
BLIGNIÈRES, FSVF

Translated by Thomas Crean, OP

AROUCA
PRESS

Originally published in French by DMM, 2019.

Copyright © Louis-Marie de Blignières, FSVF 2022
Translation © Thomas Crean, OP 2022

All rights reserved:
No part of this book may be reproduced or transmitted,
in any form or by any means, without permission

ISBN: 978-1-990685-37-8 (pbk)
ISBN: 978-1-990685-38-5 (hc)

Arouca Press
PO Box 55003
Bridgeport PO
Waterloo, ON N2J 3G0
Canada
www.aroucapress.com
Send inquiries to info@aroucapress.com

TABLE OF CONTENTS

Introduction   1

1. Are the Gospels Historically Reliable?   5
2. Is Jesus the Messiah Foretold by the Prophets?   35
3. Do the Miracles of Christ Prove His Divinity?   67
4. Does the Excellence of Christian Doctrine
   Show Its Divine Origin?   99
5. Is the Resurrection of Christ a Proof of Christianity?   135
6. Jesus's Self-Description:
   A Sign of His Divine Mission?   154

Conclusion   170

Appendix   175

About the Author   177

INTRODUCTION

THIS BOOK IS, UNASHAMEDLY, A WORK OF apologetics. I say 'unashamedly', since there is a tendency today to give a pejorative sense to this word. Apologetics is seen as a form of imprudent proselytism by which someone tries to force his interlocutor to give intellectual assent to religious belief, even though religion is, supposedly, either wholly a matter of feeling, or else depends on a purely personal decision of conscience. For many Christians, also, 'apologetics' has the undesirable connotation of an attempt to justify by reason a faith which is a pure gift of God. On this view, any attempt to prove the credibility of the faith is a form of rationalism. "There are also signs of a resurgence of *fideism*, which fails to recognize the importance of rational knowledge and philosophical discourse for the understanding of faith, indeed for the very possibility of belief in God. "[1]

Here we should briefly define what we mean by apologetics. It is the rational defence of divine revelation. In Greek, *apologia* means 'defence'. Apologetics is a part of sacred theology, that part which studies revealed religion *under the aspect of its credibility*—its aptitude to be reasonably believed—by natural reason. Yet it performs its task under the guidance of supernatural faith.

Apologetics is not, even in principle, sufficient by itself to bring someone to faith, a fact confirmed by daily experience. Nor is the science of apologetics necessary for every individual. It is, however, necessary for the Church as a whole: the Church must possess a logical set of arguments, which anyone may consult, and which can answer the questions put to her by all those who seek the truth.

At a time when Christianity is waning, apologetics is of

---

[1] Pope John Paul II, encyclical letter *Fides et ratio*, 14th September, 1998, n. 55.

great use both to pastors and to all the faithful, in particular so that they may respond to the 'dictatorship of relativism' under which they live, and so that they may aid the preaching of the gospel in formerly Christian countries.

> Consider, for example, [writes John Paul II] the natural knowledge of God, the possibility of distinguishing divine revelation from other phenomena or the recognition of its credibility, the capacity of human language to speak in a true and meaningful way even of things which transcend all human experience. From all these truths, the mind is led to acknowledge the existence of a truly propaedeutic path to faith, one which can lead to the acceptance of revelation without in any way compromising the principles and autonomy of the mind itself.[2]

The proofs that I shall propose make use of the kind of evidence employed by historians, namely texts whose authenticity is beyond doubt, and witnesses who enjoy sufficient marks of credibility. It is, however, important to bear in mind that in historical questions, proofs are not of a mathematical kind, but rest rather on probabilities or on moral certainties. Again, I deliberately put forward arguments in summary fashion, giving references to the more specialised works which elaborate them in greater detail.[3]

I do not intend to solve all possible difficulties. In particular, a detailed reply to the many recent attacks on the credibility of Christianity is beyond the scope of the present work.[4] I shall discuss only the main *arguments* on which objections to Christianity are based. To want to do away with

---

2 *Fides et ratio*, 67.
3 In my opinion, the most complete work of apologetics currently available is that of Rev. Bernard Lucien, *Apologétique. La crédibilité de la révélation divine transmise aux hommes par Jésus-Christ*. It is number 3 in the series 'Théologie sacrée pour débutants et initiés' (Nuntiavit: Brannay, 2011). It is reviewed by Leo Elders in *Sedes Sapientiae*, n. 120, pp. 103–11.
4 For a philosophically sophisticated, yet accessible, response to the so-called 'new atheism' in general, see Edward Feser, *The Last Superstition*, St Augustine's Press, 2010. For a reply to Richard Dawkins' anti-religious writing, see Thomas Crean, *God is no delusion*, Ignatius Press, 2007.

all difficulties, and with that element of mystery which, even when divine revelation is not in question, as it were enfolds our created, human condition, would be to set oneself up as God. Speaking of faith, John Henry Newman famously said: "Ten thousand difficulties do not make one doubt".[5] On the other hand, when someone puts forward rational objections, it is possible and often helpful to reply to them. When we ask our opponent to express his objection in a rational form, he often becomes less impassioned, and freer from certain prejudices which have their basis merely in the emotions. When someone becomes in this way more docile to reason, he will no longer speak at random. He will proceed rationally; or, if he does not, he will be seen to be at fault, either in the facts that he alleges or in the inferences that he draws.

---

5 *Apologia pro vita sua*, quoted by the *Catechism of the Catholic Church* (hereafter CCC) 157.

CHAPTER 1

Are the Gospels historically reliable?

IN THIS CHAPTER I SHALL CONSIDER ONE of the fundamental questions of apologetics, namely, the historical reliability of the New Testament. I shall consider principally the historicity of the gospels, since among the books reckoned as 'canonical' by Christians, it is the gospels, along with the Acts of the Apostles, which are most used to prove the fact of Christian revelation. We shall look at these texts not in the light of faith, but in the light of reason. We shall thus not be treating them as inspired texts, since belief in inspiration depends on faith.

> Those divinely revealed realities which are contained and presented in Sacred Scripture have been committed to writing under the inspiration of the Holy Spirit. For holy mother Church, relying on the belief of the Apostles (cf. John 20:31; 2 Tim. 3:16; 2 Peter 1:19–20, 3:15–16), holds that the books of both the Old and New Testaments in their entirety, with all their parts, are sacred and canonical because written under the inspiration of the Holy Spirit, they have God as their author and have been handed on as such to the Church herself. In composing the sacred books, God chose men and while employed by Him they made use of their powers and abilities, so that with Him acting in them and through them, they, as true authors, consigned to writing everything and only those things which He wanted.[1]

Our discussion seeks to show to a non-believer that the fact of supernatural revelation is attested by reliable sources.

---

1 2nd Vatican Council, Dogmatic constitution on revelation (*Dei verbum*), 11, making reference in particular to Leo XIII's encyclical letter *Providentissimus Deus*, 18th November, 1893.

SECTION I

The text and the witnesses

I. THE TEXT OF THE NEW TESTAMENT

Impartial investigation shows that the New Testament enjoys an exceptionally good historical attestation, both from the number and the antiquity of the manuscripts which we possess, and from the evidence of the authenticity and integrity of the text that we use.

A. The manuscripts

We possess a very great number of manuscripts of the New Testament. In 1986, the total was reckoned as 5,364 Greek manuscripts, ranging from the 1st to the 6th century.[2] About 36,000 quotations from the New Testament are also found in the writings of the Fathers of the Church. 53 codices contain the entire New Testament, of which the most ancient are *Vaticanus*[3] and *Sinaiticus*[4], from the 4th century.

A codex is the forerunner of the modern book, being composed, like a book, of sheets bound together. This format, which allows one to move more easily from one place in a work to another, superseded the older format, that of the scroll. In a scroll, the sheets are joined end-to-end and fixed to two rods, so that to find a given place in a document, one must unroll one end and roll up the other.

Very many papyri[5] of the 2nd and 3rd centuries give us

---

[2] 88 papyri, 274 uncial codices, 2,795 codices in minuscule, and 2,207 lectionaries. Cf. Léon Vaganay and Christian-Bernard Amphoux, *Initiation a la critique textuelle du Nouveau Testament* (Cerf: Paris, 1986). When languages other than Greek are included, it is estimated that 13,000 manuscripts containing the 27 books of the New Testament are extant. By way of comparison, only 9 or 10 manuscripts of Caesar's *Gallic Wars* exist, of which the oldest date from AD 850, that is, some 900 years later than the original text.
[3] Designated as B.03 and kept in the Vatican library in Rome.
[4] Designated as S.01 (formerly ℵ), and kept in the British Museum in London.
[5] The papyrus is the forerunner of modern paper. It was made by the Egyptians from a plant that grows on the banks of the Nile, and replaced the clay tablets formerly in use.

fragments which agree with the codices, for example p^{52} (Rylands 457), c. 125 AD, which contains a fragment of the gospel of St John (Jn. 18:31–33 and 37–38); p^{66} (Bodmer II), c. 200 AD, composed of 108 sheets including a large part of the first chapters of St John (Jn 1:1–7:53 and 8:12–14:26); and p^{45}, from the start of the 3rd century, composed of 30 sheets containing many parts of the gospels and the Acts of the Apostles.

The oldest complete manuscripts of the New Testament thus date to less than 300 years after the facts reported by them (and to an even shorter period since these facts were first written down), while the oldest fragments date to probably thirty years after the events. By comparison, for Homer, some 1,800 years intervene between the original writing and the oldest, complete manuscript in existence;[6] for Aeschylus the gap is 1500 years; for Tacitus, it is 1400 years; for Plato, 1300 years; for Julius Caesar, 1,000; and for Virgil, 800.

In regard therefore both to the number of textual witnesses to the original documents and their proximity to these documents, the New Testament surpasses all other literature of antiquity:

> Both the quantity and the quality of the manuscripts that we possess for the texts of the New Testament, and especially for the gospels, including incomplete manuscripts and fragments, far surpass what we have of the classic works of Greek and Latin antiquity.[7]

B. *Their history: authenticity and integrity*

The New Testament has come down to us at least substantially intact. This is shown by the substantial agreement of our text with the earliest sources, and by the examination of the variations in the tradition.

---

6 Namely, a Byzantine manuscript of the 10th century. A fragment of the poet's work, dating to the 4th century BC, or some 400 years later than the original, is also said to have been found in Egypt.

7 B. Lucien, *Apologétique. La crédibilité de la révélation divine transmise aux hommes par Jésus-Christ*, no. 3 in the series 'Théologie sacrée pour débutants et initiés' (Nuntiavit: Brannay, 2011).

A) AGREEMENT BETWEEN THE VERSIONS. We may mention first an indirect sign of the authenticity of the text of the New Testament: the discovery at Qumran in 1947 of a version of the text of Isaiah, dated to before AD 66, which agrees both with the version of Isaiah referred to by the two oldest codices of the whole of the New Testament (*Vaticanus* and *Sinaiticus*), and with that in our modern Christian bibles.

Next, we may follow a 'regressive' method, by starting from the texts which we possess today and working back to the oldest witnesses. Our present texts agree with the oldest manuscripts of the Latin Vulgate, those of the 6th to the 8th centuries, of which the most important are the *Codex Sangallensis*, c. 500, which contains half of the gospels, and the *Codex Fuldensis*, written between 541 and 546, which contains the whole of the New Testament. Our texts agree also with the most important ancient Greek manuscripts, in particular with those of the 4th century, *Siniaticus* and *Vaticanus*. They agree, too, with the countless quotations made by the Fathers of the Church in the 3rd and 4th centuries; with the ancient Syriac translation, used by St Aphraates (died around 367) and by St Ephraem (died in 373);[8] and with the Latin versions anterior to the Vulgate, such as the *Afra*, which Tertullian and St Cyprian used in the 2nd and 3rd centuries, and the *Itala*.

B) THE APOSTOLIC REVERENCE FOR TRADITION. Again, it is not possible that significant corruption of texts took place in the 1st century or in the course of the 2nd century. The churches at that time were engaged in a struggle against heretics, and thus took care to transmit the primitive teaching, which had been distorted by the innovators, in an

---

8 The Syrian translation was produced the year 200 on the basis of the *Diatessaron* of Tatian (a disciple of St Justin), and is preserved in codices of the 4th–5th centuries, namely *Syro-Curetonianus*, in the British Museum, and *Syro sinaiticus*, in the monastery of St Catherine of Sinai. The *Diatessaron*, a harmony of the four gospels, is found in Latin in *Codex Fuldensis*, and is reckoned to be a witness which is older than our oldest manuscripts.

unchanged form. They insisted that the faithful avoid any novelty in doctrinal matters, showing that they had a very great reverence for apostolic tradition.

This reverence for tradition, in fact, goes back to the earliest times, as can be seen from the oldest parts of the New Testament, the letters of St Paul. We may consider the following examples: "As for a factious[9] man, after a first and a second warning, separate yourselves from him" (Titus 3:10); "when you had received of us the word of the hearing of God, you received it not as the word of men, but (as it is indeed) the word of God, who worketh in you that have believed. For you, brethren, are become followers of the churches of God which are in Judea, in Christ Jesus" (1 Thess. 2:13–14); "I wonder that you are so soon removed from him that called you into the grace of Christ, unto another gospel. Which is not another, only there are some that trouble you, and would pervert the gospel of Christ. But though we, or an angel from heaven, preach a gospel to you besides that which we have preached to you, let him be anathema." (Gal. 1:6–8); "But thanks be to God, that you were the servants of sin, but have obeyed from the heart, unto that form of doctrine, into which you have been delivered. [. . .] I beseech you, brethren, to mark them who make dissensions and offences contrary to the doctrine which you have learned, and avoid them" (Rom. 6:17 and 16:17).

The same reverence for tradition is found with the other apostles. St John says: "If any man come to you, and bring not this doctrine, receive him not into the house nor say to him, God speed you" (2 Jn. 10). St Peter writes: "There were also false prophets among the people, even as there shall be among you lying teachers, who shall bring in sects of perdition, and deny the Lord who bought them: bringing upon themselves swift destruction" (2 Pet. 2:1). St Jude says:

---

9 The Vulgate reads *hereticum hominem*, following the Greek *aireticon anthrôpon*. The phrase is sometimes translated as 'heretic', or 'a man who causes divisions', in accordance with the etymology of the Greek word, which is literally 'one who chooses' (in matters of doctrine).

CHRISTIANITY IS CREDIBLE

"Dearly beloved, taking all care to write unto you concerning your common salvation, I was under a necessity to write unto you: to beseech you to contend earnestly for the faith once delivered to the saints. For certain men are secretly entered in, (who were written of long ago unto this judgment), ungodly men, turning the grace of our Lord God into riotousness, and denying the only sovereign Ruler, and our Lord Jesus Christ. [..] But you, my dearly beloved, be mindful of the words which have been spoken before by the apostles of our Lord Jesus Christ, who told you, that in the last time there should come mockers, walking according to their own desires in ungodlinesses. These are they, who separate themselves, sensual men, having not the Spirit" (Jude 3–4, 17–19).

C) REVERENCE FOR TRADITION AMONG THE APOSTOLIC FATHERS. The non-canonical writings produced by the first Fathers of the Church also insist on the need to have a strict regard for the tradition of the apostles. St Ignatius of Antioch, the disciple of St Polycarp of Smyrna, who had himself known St John, writes as follows:

> I have learned that certain men, coming from there, came to you bringing an evil teaching; but you did not let them sow any seed among you, for you blocked your ears so as not to receive what they were sowing. You kept in mind that you are stones of the temple of the Father, made ready for the building of God the Father, lifted on high by that engine of Jesus Christ which is the Cross, holding yourselves as the cable of the Holy Ghost. Your faith draws you on high, and charity is the path that leads you up toward God.[10]

Clement of Rome, who was one of the first popes, and who died around the year 100, wrote thus:

> If we have written all this to you, beloved, it is not only as a warning for you, but also as a reminder for ourselves, since we have entered the same arena and

---

10 Ignatius of Antioch, *Letter to the Ephesians*, 9.1; Rouet de Journel [*RJ*] 40.

await the same combat as you. So let us leave behind vain and useless cares and adapt ourselves to the glorious and venerable rules of our tradition. Let us look to what is good, well-pleasing, and acceptable to him who made us.[11]

In one of the oldest of the non-canonical writings, the *Didache* or *Teaching of the Twelve Apostles*, we read: "Thou shalt never abandon the commandments of the Lord, but thou shalt guard those things which thou hast received, adding nothing and taking nothing away."[12]

We should note that all these texts quickly became known to the pastors and the faithful, thanks to the preaching of the apostles and their first disciples. The fact that the churches were everywhere on their guard against innovations, and distrusted apocryphal writings, makes it highly unlikely that the canonical writings could have been replaced by non-canonical ones.

D) A LIMITED NUMBER OF IMPORTANT VARIATIONS. Whilst there are certainly a large number of variant readings in the manuscripts (between 150,000 and 250,000, or about 1/60th of the whole), very few of them affect the meaning of the text. Those that do affect it number about 200, of which only about fifteen are of any great importance: about 150 words out of the 150,000 words of the New Testament. This comes to only 1/1000th part of the whole, a marked contrast with any of the profane works of the ancient world.[13] Textual criticism, moreover, often enables us to establish the correct reading. The few variant readings which affect the meaning do not introduce any new doctrinal truths not contained elsewhere; nor do they reject any doctrines; nor do they give a different account of the historical facts.

---

11 Clement of Rome, *First Letter to the Corinthians*, 7.
12 *Didache*, 4.13; *RJ* 2.
13 "All other books, whether profane or ecclesiastical, have come down to us in only a few, late codices; in almost all cases with no ancient translation, and rarely quoted by ancient writers" (Vaccari, *Instit. Biblicae*, I, 3, 2, n. 54).

II. THE WITNESSES

A. *The Christian witnesses*

The authenticity of the gospels is corroborated both by St Paul and by the Fathers.

1. ST PAUL. The information contained in certain of the letters of the Apostle to the Gentiles is all the more valuable in that the authenticity of these letters is accepted by everyone. They are the first epistle to the Thessalonians (50–51), the epistle to the Philippians (56), the epistle to the Galatians (56–57), the two epistles to the Corinthians (56 and 57), and the epistle to the Romans (57–58). These letters were written twenty to thirty years after the death of Christ. While they do not contain an extended account of the life of Jesus, they set forth its overall form and its main characteristics, and they do so with precision, speaking of it as something which is certain.

Jesus had a Jewish mother, and lived in accordance with the law (Gal. 4:4). He had relations and came of ancient Jewish stock (1 Cor. 9:5; Rom. 9:3–5). He was a son of David and of Abraham (Rom. 1:3; Gal. 3:16). He lived as a poor man (2 Cor. 8:9; Phil. 2:7). He established a college of twelve apostles (1 Cor. 9:5, 15:5). He instituted the Eucharist on the night that he was handed over (1 Cor. 11:23–26). He was sacrificed (1 Cor. 5:7; Gal. 2:20) by crucifixion (1 Cor. 1:17, 1:23, 2:2, 8; 2 Cor. 13:4; Gal. 3:13). He died and was buried (Rom. 5:6ff, 6:3–10, 8:34, 14:9; 1 Cor. 15:3–4; 1 Thess. 2:15, 4:14). He rose again (1 Cor. 15:4ff; Rom. 1:4, 4:25, 8:34; 1 Thess. 1:10, 4:14). He was seen by his disciples after his resurrection (1 Cor. 15: 5–8; 9:1).

All these statements agree perfectly with what we are told by the gospels.

2. THE FIRST FATHERS OF THE CHURCH. The Fathers of the Church speak in numerous places about the gospels and the Acts of the Apostles and give us information about their authors. I shall mention only the most ancient references, those from the 2nd and 3rd centuries, and especially ones

taken from those men who, since they knew the immediate disciples of the apostles, are called the 'apostolic fathers'.

St Ignatius of Antioch, who died in 107, wrote in his *Letter to the Philadelphians*:

> I exhort you to do nothing in a quarrelsome way, but everything according to Christ's teaching. I have heard some men who say: "If I cannot find it in the records, I will not believe it in the gospel."[14] And when I said to them: "It is written down", they replied: "That is what is in question." For my part, my records are Jesus Christ: the inviolable records are his cross, his death, his resurrection, and the faith that comes from him. It is by this that I hope to be justified, with the help of your prayers.[15]

Papias was the bishop of Hierapolis in the 2nd century. Here are the statements made by him around the year 130, as reported by Eusebius of Caesarea:

> This is what the elder said: "Mark, who was Peter's interpreter, wrote down carefully, though not at Peter's bidding, everything which Peter remembered as having been said or done by the Lord. For Mark himself had not heard or followed the Lord; it was only later on, as I have said, that he followed Peter. Peter used to give his teachings as occasion arose, rather than producing a single account of the words of the Lord. In this way, Mark made no errors, since he wrote what Peter remembered. He had, in fact, no other aim than to leave out nothing of what he had heard, nor to err in anything that he reported." That is what Papias said of Mark. In regard to Matthew, he said: "Matthew compiled the *logia* [the words of Jesus] in Hebrew, and various people translated them as they were able."[16]

The *Muratorian fragment* provides an important confirmation of the fact that the books of the New Testament were

---

14   Alternative translation: "If I cannot find it in the records, that is, in the gospels, I will not believe it."
15   Ignatius of Antioch, *Ad Philadelphenses*, 8.2; *RJ* 60.
16   Eusebius of Caesarea, *Ecclesiastical History*, 3.39.5; *RJ* 95.

known to the churches at a very early date and accepted by them as authentic. This document is a Latin manuscript dating to the 7th or 8th century, which was discovered in the 18th century in the Ambrosian library in Milan by an Italian historian named Luigi-Antonio Muratori. It is a translation of a Greek original which has been dated with certainty to about the year 107. Although the beginning and ending of this text are missing, it mentions Luke and John, described respectively as the 3rd and 4th gospels.

St Irenaeus, bishop of Lyons, wrote his *Treatise against heresies* between the years 180 and 185. He says:

> Matthew, then, produced for the Hebrews a written form of the gospel, in their own language, at the time when Peter and Paul were preaching in Rome and founding the church there. After they had died, Mark, the disciple and interpreter of Peter, also passed on to us Peter's preaching, in written form. Luke, Paul's companion, wrote down in a book what Paul had preached. Then John also, the disciple of the Lord, the one who had rested on his breast, wrote his gospel while he lived at Ephesus, in the province of Asia. [...]
>
> The authority which these gospels enjoy is so great that even the heretics recognise them, and so try to pull some shred out of them in support of their own teaching. Thus, the Ebionites use only the gospel of Matthew; and yet this very gospel convicts them of thinking wrongly of the Lord. Marcion does violence to the gospel of Luke, but the fragments which he keeps show that he is a blasphemer in regard to the one true God. Those who divide Jesus from Christ, and claim that Christ did not suffer, but only Jesus, make much of the gospel according to Mark; yet if only they read it with love for the truth, they would be able to return to a healthy way of thinking.[17]

Around the year 207, Tertullian, in his *Treatise against Marcion*, wrote:

---

[17] Irenaeus of Lyons, *Against the Heresies*, 3.1.1 and 3.1.17; *RJ* 208 and 214.

We set this down as a first principle: the record of the gospels derives from the apostles. It is they to whom the Lord himself gave the task of making known the gospel. If there were also some apostolic persons who were their authors, they did not act of themselves, but with and after the apostles. The preaching of disciples might be suspected to arise out of a desire for fame, if it had not been supported by the authority of their masters, or rather by that of Christ, who gave them apostles to be their masters. Among the apostles, it is John and Matthew who give to us our faith; and among the apostolic men, it is Luke and Mark who renew it for us. They all started with the same principles of faith, in regard to the one God the Creator, and to his Christ, who was born of the Virgin and fulfilled the law and the prophets.[18]

Around 244, Origen wrote in his *Commentary on St Matthew*:

About the four gospels, the only ones about which there is no dispute in the Church of God on earth, I have learned from tradition that the first is that written by Matthew, who had been a tax-collector and became an apostle of Jesus Christ. He wrote it in Hebrew for the believers who had come out of Judaism. The second is that according to Mark, who produced it in accordance with what Peter had shown him. Peter, in fact, calls him his son in his Catholic epistle, where he says: "The chosen Church which is in Babylon greets you, as does Mark, my son." The third gospel is that according to Luke, which is praised by Paul, and written for the converts from among the gentiles. Finally, the gospel according to John.[19]

Eusebius of Caesarea records a fragment of Clement of Alexandria's work *Hypotyposes*:

In the same books, Clement again sets forth the tradition of the ancient presbyters about the order of the gospels, as follows. He says that the gospels which contain

---
18 Tertullian, *Adversus Marcion*, 4.2.1 and 4.2.2; *RJ* 339.
19 Reported by Eusebius of Caesarea in *Ecclesiastical History*, 6.25.4–6; *RJ* 503.

genealogies were written before the others. Mark's came to be written like this: Peter used to preach the word of God publicly in Rome, and expounded the gospel under the inspiration of the Spirit; those who had been present at his preaching, a large number of people, encouraged Mark, as having been for a long time the companion of Peter and as one who remembered what he had said, to write it all down. He did so, and gave the gospel to the people who had asked him for it. Peter learned of the project, without either advising that it be stopped, or encouraging it.

It was, however, John, urged by the disciples and divinely inspired by the Spirit, who saw that the material side of things had been explained by the other gospels, and so he wrote a spiritual gospel.[20]

B. Non-Christian witnesses

1. WITNESSES FROM THE JEWISH WORLD. Flavius Josephus (37–105), an eye-witness of the Jewish War, was very well-versed both in the Jewish culture and religion from which he came, and also in Roman affairs, since he eventually transferred his allegiance to the empire. Writing around the year 93, he makes reference to John the Baptist.

Now, certain Jews believed that Herod's army had been destroyed by the will of God as a just punishment for John, called the Baptist. For Herod had had him killed, even though he had been a just man who had roused the Jews to the practice of virtue, telling them to be just toward each other, and devout toward God, so as to receive baptism.[21]

Josephus also speaks of James, the 'brother' of Jesus:

Ananias [the high priest] was one of these [a member of the party of the Sadducees]. Seeing a favourable opportunity, with Festus being dead, and Albinus [the procurator named for Judaea] still travelling, he called together the Sanhedrin. He handed over to it James, brother of Jesus who is called Christ, as well as certain

---

20 Eusebius of Caesarea, *Ecclesiastical History*, 6.14.5–7; *RJ* 439.
21 Flavius Josephus, *On the Antiquities of the Jews*, 18.5

others, and accusing them of having transgressed the Law, he had them stoned.[22]

One passage in Josephus which speaks about Christ (the so-called *testimonium flavianum*)[23] has been the subject of much discussion. It appears that an uninterpolated Arabic translation of it was discovered in 1971 by Shlomo Pinès, a professor at the Hebrew University of Jerusalem, in the *Universal History* of Agapius, a bishop of Hierapolis in Syria in the 10th century.

> At this time there was a wise man who was called Jesus. His conduct was good, and [he] was known to be virtuous. And many people from among the Jews and the other nations became his disciples. Pilate condemned him to be crucified and to die. But those who had become his disciples did not abandon his discipleship. They reported that he had appeared to them three days after his crucifixion, and that he was alive; accordingly he was perhaps the Messiah concerning whom the prophets have recounted wonders.[24]

The ancient Jewish sources are the Mishna and the Talmud. The Mishna is a collection of the traditional laws and customs of the Pharisees' schools, written down toward the end of the 2nd century of our era. The Talmud is a commentary on the Mishna and exists in a Palestinian version of the 4th century (the Jerusalem Talmud), and a Babylonian version of the 5th century (the Babylonian Talmud). These sources contain few useful historical elements and engage in a harsh polemic against Jesus. However, it is noteworthy that although they mischaracterise his life, they provide several facts that agree with the narrative of the gospels; in fact, according to the Jewish author Joseph Klausner, in a book that marks a change of perspective of Judaism toward Jesus, they do not dispute the historical character of the gospels.[25]

---

22 Ibid. 20.9
23 Ibid. 18.3
24 Cf. *International Herald Tribune*, 14th February, 1972: "Jews bring historical proofs of Jesus's existence".
25 Joseph Klausner, *Jésus de Nazareth, son temps, sa vie, sa doctrine*, Paris, 1933.

CHRISTIANITY IS CREDIBLE

2. PAGAN WITNESSES. Testimonies to Jesus are found in some important secular authors of the 1st and 2nd century. Tacitus, the disciple of Pliny the Elder, was in Judaea in the time of Titus. In his Annals, written between 69 and 117, he speaks of the fire of Rome, under Nero. He affirms:

> In order to quell the rumours, [Nero] accused the Christians, who were hated for their abominable practices, of being guilty, and he punished them with all kinds of appalling tortures. The name Christian comes from Chrestus, who was put to death by Pontius Pilate, procurator of Judaea in the reign of Tiberius.[26]

Pliny the Younger, the governor of Bithynia in Asia Minor, wrote to the emperor Trajan in about 112 concerning the spread of Christianity in his province. He asks for instructions about the policy to adopt in regard to this group:

> They say that their only crime or error is that they are accustomed to gather on a fixed day, before sunrise, to sing hymns alternately[27] to Christ as to a god, and to undertake by solemn oaths not to commit any evil deed. A host of people of every age and condition have been accused, both men and women. [...] This contagious superstition has not infected the cities only; it has spread into the smaller towns and into the heart of the countryside. [...] Crowds now begin to return to our temples, which had previously been almost abandoned. [...] You will gather how many miscreants it should be possible to recall to their duties.[28]

Around the year 120, in his *Lives of the Twelve Caesars*, Suetonius writes: "[Claudius] expelled the Jews from Rome, since under the influence of one Chrestus, they had become a permanent cause of disorder."[29] The Acts of the Apostles make an allusion to the expulsion: "After these things, departing

---

26 Tacitus, *Annales*, III.XV.44.
27 *Secum invicem*—this may refer to the practice of two 'choirs' which sing alternate parts of the chant.
28 Pliny the Younger, *Epistulae*, X.97.
29 Suetonius, *Vita Claudii*, XXV.4. Claudius was emperor from 41 to 52.

from Athens, he came to Corinth. And finding a certain Jew, named Aquila, born in Pontus, lately come from Italy, with Priscilla his wife, (because that Claudius had commanded all Jews to depart from Rome,) he came to them" (Acts 18:1–2).

Speaking of Nero, Suetonius records that he "punished the Christians, a group that followed a new and dangerous superstition".[30]

St Justin states that the imperial *Acta* of events described by the gospel existed in Rome in the 2nd century:

> It was also predicted that Jesus Christ would heal the sick and raise the dead. Listen: "At his arrival, the lame will leap like a deer, and the tongue of the mute will be eloquent; the blind will see, and lepers made clean, and the dead will stand up and walk." The Acts of Pontius Pilate offer you a proof of all these facts.[31]

SECTION II

The historical value of the New Testament

THE HISTORICAL VALUE OF THE NEW TEStament may be established directly, by considering whether the texts of the New Testament satisfy the criteria of historicity. It can also be confirmed indirectly, by showing how none of the alternative explanations is possible.

I. THE DIRECT PROOF

As mentioned above, certitude in historical matters is something moral rather than mathematical. With this in mind, we can say that the texts of the New Testament fulfil the conditions necessary for 'historical faith' to be accorded to a given writing. Namely:

(1) They belong to the literary genre of genuine history;
(2) Their authors are well-informed;
(3) Their authors are truthful.

---

30 Suetonius, *Vita Neronis*, XVI.2
31 Justin, *Apology*, I.48.

CHRISTIANITY IS CREDIBLE

A. The literary genre of the texts

When one reads the gospels, it is easy to distinguish passages of an allegorical nature, such as the parables, or poetic passages, such as the *Benedictus* of Zechariah and Mary's *Magnificat*, from the account of the Lord's life and words. His life and words are recounted in the form usual for a historical narrative, giving the names of identifiable historical personages, and with specific dates and times. The gospels are not written in an atemporal manner, like a legend beginning with the words, "Once upon a time in a far-off land..." For example, the gospel according to St John includes a great many precise details about times, places, circumstances and customs. The evangelists speak always in a sober, unrhetorical manner, even when they are mentioning sublime things. Their style is simple and objective. There are no myths or absurd or fanciful exaggerations, as one does find throughout the apocryphal gospels, which were current in the 2nd century, and which belong to the genre of popular, and not strictly historical, literature. We might say that the apocryphal gospels exemplify the 'Law of the Growth of Myths', that is, the common tendency for people to give free rein to their imagination when speaking of the lives of great men, after their deaths.

The objective, and historical character of the gospels, even when they speak of miracles, is something so obvious that it was acknowledged by all the ancient writers. Among friendly witnesses, Irenaeus, Clement of Alexandria and Origen, though otherwise very ready to discover allegories in Scripture, fully admit the historicity of the gospels. But the same is true even on the part of Christianity's early enemies. Celsus, for example, whose anti-Christian polemic has won him the title of 'the pagan Voltaire',[32] or 'the Voltaire of the 2nd century'[33], did not deny the miracles of Jesus, but simply

---

[32] "Celsus, [...] set on mockery and insults, is the Voltaire of Paganism, while Porphyry is its Renan", Paul Allard, *La persecution de Dioclétien et le triomphe de l'Église*, vol. 1, Paris, Gabalda, 1908, p. 74.
[33] H. Pillard de La Boullaye, *Jésus et l'histoire*, Conférences de Notre-Dame de Paris (Année 1929), Paris, Editions Spes, 1929, p. 46.

took them for the marvellous deeds of a magician.[34] Porphyry, the great neo-Platonic philosopher, sought to account for the whole of Jesus's work in a rationalist manner.[35]

The gospels are clearly not a biography of Jesus in the modern sense, complete with footnotes, bibliography and references to archives. But they nevertheless belong to a literary genre which intends *carefully to recount events which really occurred*. St Luke, in fact, explicitly states this at the start of his gospel: "Forasmuch as many have taken in hand to set forth in order a narration of the things that have been accomplished among us; according as they have delivered them unto us, who from the beginning were eyewitnesses and ministers of the word: it seemed good to me also, having diligently (*akribôs*) attained to all things from the beginning, to write to thee in order, most excellent Theophilus, that thou mayest know the verity (*tèn asphaleian*) of those words in which thou hast been instructed. " (Lk 1:1–4). The infancy narratives are also genuinely historical, even though written in a style proper to biblical religious history.[36] Benedict XVI, writing as a private theologian, remarked:

> Matthew and Luke, each in his own way, wished not only to tell 'a story', but *to write a true history of what took place*, albeit a history interpreted and understand by means of the word of God. This means that they didn't intend to write a full account, but only to note what seemed important in the light of the Word, and for the new community of faith.[37]

B. *The authors were well-informed*

The authors of the New Testament were, in the case of Matthew, Peter and John, immediate witnesses to the facts, and, in the case of Mark, Luke and Paul, intimately acquainted

---

34 Cf. Origen, *Contra Celsum*, 1.68.
35 Cf. St Jerome, *Liber hebraicarum quaestionum in Genesim*, 1.10.
36 Cf. René Laurentin, *Structure et théologie de Luc I–II*, 2 tomes, Paris, Gabalda, 1957.
37 Joseph Ratzinger—Benedict XVI, *L'enfance de Jésus*, Paris, Flammarion, 2012, p. 32 (italics added).

with immediate witnesses such as the Blessed Virgin Mary, the apostles and the other disciples. We have already seen the words of Papias of Hierapolis in regard to Mark: "Mark, who was Peter's interpreter, wrote down carefully (*akribôs*) [...]". This statement is confirmed by the words of St Irenaeus, Origen and Clement of Alexandria. Paul consulted the apostles and James, the 'brother of the Lord' (Gal. 1–2). As for Luke, it was only after "having informed himself accurately about everything since the beginning" that he undertook his "orderly" account of the facts, relying on eye-witnesses, as also those who had written before him had done, "in accordance with what the men who from the start were eye-witnesses and servants of the word have transmitted to us" (Lk. 1:2–3).

As Father Lagrange explains:

> Those who were part of the same group as Luke [Luke says, "in accordance with what has been transmitted to us (èmin)"] were among those who had heard the first witnesses, and who had written their accounts on that basis [...] Luke had the right to seek to produce something better than his predecessors, and would hardly have set about his work without such an intention. He does not, however, find any fault with them. Yet having the inclination for this kind of work, and the opportunity to carry it out, he considered that he had the right to attempt it. Given his concern for historical accuracy, he could not fail to make use of what had been written previously.[38]

Without entering into the debate in detail, we can note that the opinion according to which the gospels were written down at any early date has been increasingly accepted over the last fifty years.[39] If such opinions are correct, then we

---

38 M.-J. Lagrange, *The Gospel according to St Luke*, pp. 4 and 6.
39 Cf. John A. T. Robinson, *Redating the New Testament*, Norwich, SCM Press, 1976–1984 ; Jean Carmignac, *La naissance des Évangiles synoptiques*, Paris, ŒIL, 1984 ; Claude Tresmontant, *Le Christ hébreu, La langue et l'âge des Évangiles*, Paris, ŒIL, 1983 ; C. P. Thiede, *Témoin de Jésus : le papyrus d'Oxford et l'origine des Évangiles*, Paris, Robert Laffont, 1996 ; Philippe Rolland, *Les premiers Évangiles : un nouveau*

can say that the evangelists wrote at a time very close to the events. According to the *Sacrae Theologiae Summa*, a theological course which was written for the Spanish Jesuits at the start of the 1960's, and which made use of the contemporary critical studies, "Matthew wrote around the year 45, Mark between 53 and 58, and Luke around 58–62".[40] Philippe Roland takes the view that Matthew, having written his gospel in Hebrew, was translated into Greek before the year 40, with Luke writing in 63 and Mark in 66–67.[41]

For his part, Frédéric Guillaud believes that we have a proof—it would be better to say 'a very strong sign'—that "the accounts date from contemporaries of Jesus, and not from editors living outside Palestine at a later date":

> If one correlates the personal names contained in the four gospels and the Acts of the Apostles against the statistical distribution of such names found at this time in this region (as research has established this distribution in the 20th century by referring to graves, Jewish historians and the Dead Sea Scrolls), one finds a remarkable correspondence. The two things tally perfectly. [...] (a hypothetical forger would not have access to indices of names, nor even to Wikipedia!) Try, by an educated guess, to produce a list of 80 persons, giving them forenames which correspond exactly to the statistical distribution of such names in any given period, including your own: you will not succeed. It's something which is almost impossible to achieve without scholarly resources.[42]

---

regard sur le problème synoptique, coll. « Lectio divina, 116 », Paris, Cerf, 1984. The citation of these works naturally does not imply agreement with all the positions contained in them. See also the Ignatius Study Bible (New Testament), edited by Scott Hahn and Curtis Mitch.
40 M. Nicolau SJ and J. Salverri SJ, *Sacrae theologiae summa*, t. 1, Madrid, Biblioteca de autores christianos [BAC], 1962, p. 258. English translation by Kenneth Baker.
41 Cf. Philippe Rolland, *L'origine de la date des Évangiles. Les témoins oculaires de Jésus*, Éditions Saint-Paul, Paris, 1994, pp. 163–64. Rolland is speaking of a primitive gospel of Matthew, written in Hebrew or Aramaic, and soon translated into Greek. He takes the view that the canonical gospel of Matthew, written directly in Greek, dates from 62 or 63.
42 Frédéric Guillaud, *Catholic reloaded....* pp. 81–82.

However, he adds:

> The hypothesis of a 'long' period of oral tradition [...] does not as such tend to put the historical reliability of these texts in doubt. On this view, the accuracy and truthfulness of these official documents is guaranteed by the apostolic Church, to which the arguments traditionally used in favour of Matthew, Mark, Luke and John [i.e., their knowledge of the facts and their good faith], would be fittingly applied.[43]

In other words, the documentary evidence shows clearly that the early Church was not at all some anarchic mix of small, charismatic groups, each drawing inspiration according to its personal taste from various myths, but rather a hierarchically structured community with the goal of preserving and handing on the word and deeds of Jesus, as guaranteed by the apostles and other living witnesses who were all imbued with an absolute respect for tradition. If the assertions recorded in the gospels had not agreed with what these witnesses had seen or heard, the churches would have protested, and would not have accepted and venerated these writings as in fact they did.[44] Paul speaks thus to Timothy his disciple: "Thou therefore, my son, be strong in the grace which is in Christ Jesus. And the things which thou hast heard of me by many witnesses, the same commend to faithful men, who shall be fit to teach others also" (2 Tim. 2:1–2).

The facts recorded in the gospels were, moreover, ones easy to observe and to express: the life of a Jewish rabbi, consisting of precise events in particular places, preaching, journeys in a small country, and spectacular deeds performed in front of numerous witnesses. The gospels are not akin to Thucydides' *History of the Peloponnesian War*, containing all the political and military complexity of a prolonged armed

---

43 B. Lucien, *Apologétique. La crédibilité...* p. 346.
44 Cf. René Latourelle SJ, *L'acces à Jésus par les Évangiles : histoire et herméneutique*, Tournay, Desclée-Montréal, Bellarmin, 1978, pp. 133–253 ; and Pierre Grelot, *passim*, especially, *L'origine des Évangiles : Controverse avec Jean Carmignac*, Paris, Cerf, 1986.

conflict between several peoples—and yet this is generally reckoned as the earliest work to offer a reliable and carefully written historical narrative. Nor are the gospels akin to Julius Caesar's *Gallic Wars*—though this work, also, is universally accepted as substantially a work of history.

Finally, the sayings of a rabbi could be faithfully preserved, even before they were written down, thanks to the Semitic practice of learning by recitation. The skills employed in such oral traditions are today increasingly understood and appreciated.[45]

C. *The truthfulness of the authors*

The truthfulness of the authors appears from the impossibility of deceit, an impossibility that derives both from the authors themselves and from their readers. This truthfulness is confirmed by an internal examination of the texts.

THE IMPOSSIBILITY OF DECEIT: THE AUTHORS. No one lies without a reason. The authors of the gospels, following the teaching of their master, disdain honours and wealth, and have no motive to lie. They had nothing to gain from inventing history, other than the disgrace of being excluded from the synagogue and suffering persecution. If they had been seeking their own advantage, they would have adapted themselves to the popular expectation of a glorious Messiah. They did just the opposite, speaking of a poor and crucified Messiah, and preaching a kingdom which is above all spiritual. They were devout, practising Jews: had they made up a history while narrating it as if it had really occurred, and depicted an imaginary prophet calling himself the 'Son of God', they would have been guilty of lying grievously about a matter of religion, and guilty also of blasphemy. Such crimes are not compatible with their piety and moral practice, as these can be known from their teaching, their life and their death.

---

45 On this subject of memorisation, cf. Marcel Jousse, *L'anthropologie du geste*, Paris, Gallimard, 1974. One could also mention Frédéric Guigain, *Exégèse d'oralité*, Paris, Cariscipt, 2011, without necessarily accepting his argument in all its details.

Jesus, the master of the evangelists, enjoined strict truthfulness upon his disciples (Matt. 5:37). The apostles and the first Christians accepted and taught this precept (Jas. 5:12; 1 Pet. 2:1), and observed it from the start of their ministry, even though it led to persecution: "For our part, we cannot but speak of what we have seen and heard" (Acts 4:20). They held that the love of the truth was a basic requirement for salvation (2 Thess. 2:8–10).

The social context created by the first Christian communities was deeply marked by a sense of truthfulness, both in general, and particularly in regard to the words and deeds of Jesus. To one who considers the matter with a critical, though not a sceptical, mind, these are the best possible conditions for establishing the historical reliability of the human witnesses.[46]

THE IMPOSSIBILITY OF DECEIT: THE READERS. At the time when the gospel was first preached, and also when the gospels were first written down, eye-witnesses to Jesus's life, both friendly and hostile, were still alive. Such witnesses could easily have exposed the evangelists if they had been guilty of lying or of fabricating events. Yet we do not find any trace of such a protest being made by any Christian; nor among the enemies of the new Christian religion do we find anyone denying that the facts recorded in the gospels are substantially accurate. On the contrary, the gospels were immediately received with religious veneration and read in all the churches by the first Christians, who had already been instructed orally by the apostles themselves or by those whom the apostles had sent. "I make known unto you, brethren, the gospel which I preached to you (*to euaggelion ho euèggelisamen humin*), which also you have received, and wherein you stand, by which also you are saved, if you hold fast after what manner I preached unto you, unless you have believed in vain. For I delivered unto you first of all, which I also received" (1 Cor. 15:1–3).

---

46 B. Lucien, *Apologétique. La crédibilité...* p. 408.

VERACITY OF THE EVANGELISTS CONFIRMED BY INTERNAL EXAMINATION OF THE GOSPELS. The geographical and historical facts about first-century Palestine, which are better established today than in the past, are faithfully reflected by the gospels, whether it be details about censuses, political authorities, religious practices, sects or local customs. The 'archaeological revolution' which has taken place over the last hundred years or so has afforded a wealth of information about Jewish and Roman society, and it confirms the accuracy of the gospel accounts. For example, in the 1960's and 1970's, the discovery of ancient inscriptions confirmed certain details whose authenticity had previously been put in doubt, such as the names 'Nazareth' and 'Pontius Pilate' (found on stones in Caesarea Maritima), the title 'proconsul' (rather than pro-praetor), as given to Sergius Paulus, the governor of Cyprus (Acts 13:7), and the title of 'politarch' given to the leading men of the city of Thessalonika (Acts 17:8).

Again, the sublime teachings of the gospel, and the unique personality of Jesus himself, could not have been simple inventions of men such as the evangelists, who had no particular status in the world of their time, nor were possessed of much literary or philosophical learning.

The only adequate explanation that one can give of the New Testament writings is thus the objective reality of the person and the events described therein. The very existence of Christianity, deriving as it does from the Gospel, would be otherwise an effect without a cause.

II. THE INDIRECT PROOF

This conclusion can be confirmed indirectly, by the impossibility of all other explanations. The philosopher Jean Guitton made a long enquiry into the riddle posed by the gospels' picture of Jesus. His researches resulted in a book entitled *Jesus*, wherein he writes as follows:

> When we study the history of the last one hundred and fifty years, we see the same themes repeating themselves.

The use of new methods makes no fundamental difference to the positions on offer, which are not many. [...] It even seems as if the more work that is done, the less anything original is said. [...] When I tried to list the various different kinds of explanation, what surprised me was how few there were. I came to think that there are and can be only three: the first two are both ways of denying the gospels, while the third alternative is to accept them.

Guitton then explained the first two hypotheses, which deny the historicity of the gospels, and he analysed the inextricable difficulties which they involve.

A. The critical hypothesis: from a man to God

This is the explanation first put forward by the great rationalists in the 18th century, and developed in the 19th and 20th centuries, especially by Renan and Loisy. It consists in seeing the birth of Christianity as a purely natural phenomenon. On this view, Jesus was a man who certainly existed (and who was perhaps exceptional), but who did nothing supernatural and was *gradually divinised* by the early community: history was turned into 'faith' by believers. On this account, the relation between historical truth and the gospels is confused and varies from one episode to another. It supposedly belongs to a 'critical reading' of the texts to discern where the early community, carried away by its 'faith', has added something to the facts.

This theory, which recognises Jesus as, at most, an outstanding Jewish prophet, does not account for the historical facts. It does not explain why he was the only one of the many 'Messiahs' of the period to have left disciples and to have made an enduring mark on history, even though he had exhibited none of the traits of the political Messiah widely expected by the Jews—an expectation which led to all the bloodshed of the Jewish wars.

The 'critical solution' is also open to other irrefutable objections. The main one is that the hypothesis of a Jew divinised by Jews is simply absurd. The idea of an incarnation of God could not have come naturally to the Jewish mind:

> During the four thousand years of the religious history of the Hebrews, not only was there never any other equally inexplicable 'divinisation' as in the case of Jesus, but also none of the disciples of any of the messiahs, however full of his new enthusiasm, ever thought even for a moment, or thought even in some limited sense, of putting his Christ on the same level as Yahweh.[47]

Here we may turn to those parts of the New Testament which are recognised, even by the critical school, as the oldest: among the gospels, St Mark's, written before AD 70;[48] among the letters of St Paul, the first epistle to the Thessalonians, written before 52;[49] the letter to the Philippians, written before 56;[50] and the first letter to the Corinthians, dated to before AD 57.[51] All these texts prove that

---

47 V. Messori, *Hypothèses sur Jésus*, p. 128.
48 "When Jesus had seen their faith, he saith to the sick of the palsy: Son, thy sins are forgiven thee. And there were some of the scribes sitting there, and thinking in their hearts: Why doth this man speak thus? He blasphemeth. *Who can forgive sins, but God only?* Which Jesus presently knowing in his spirit, that they so thought within themselves, saith to them: Why think you these things in your hearts? Which is easier, to say to the sick of the palsy: Thy sins are forgiven thee; or to say: Arise, take up thy bed, and walk? But *that you may know that the Son of man hath power on earth to forgive sins,* (he saith to the sick of the palsy,) I say to thee: Arise, take up thy bed, and go into thy house. And immediately he arose; and taking up his bed, went his way in the sight of all; so that all wondered and glorified God, saying: We never saw the like" (Mk 2:5–12).
49 "God hath not appointed us unto wrath, but unto the purchasing of salvation by our Lord Jesus Christ, *who died for us;* that, whether we watch or sleep, we may live together with him" (1 Thess. 5:9–10).
50 "Who being in the form of God, thought it not robbery to be equal with God: but emptied himself, taking the form of a servant, being made in the likeness of men, and in habit found as a man. He humbled himself, becoming obedient unto death, even to the death of the cross. For which cause God also hath exalted him, and hath given him a name which is above all names, that in the name of Jesus every knee should bow, of those that are in heaven, on earth, and under the earth, and that every tongue should confess that the Lord Jesus Christ is in the glory of God the Father" (Phil 2: 6–11).
51 "I delivered unto you first of all, which I also received: how that Christ died for our sins, according to the scriptures: and that he was

in the original preaching (the 'kerygma'), Jesus was *from the beginning* believed and declared to possess the prerogatives of God, especially those of freeing people from their sins, granting salvation, and raising the dead.

If the first preachers of the gospel had set out to 'divinise a mere man', then they would have needed not only a fertile imagination, but also great boldness; more than anyone else in history. Yet considered from this point of view, they say either too much or too little. They say too much, insofar as they give an unvarnished account of their own failings and faults, especially of the scandalous betrayal of Jesus by Peter, the leader of their group. They portray Peter, though a key figure, as denying his master three times, not because he is being pressurised by an intimidating court of law, but while talking to some servants warming themselves at a fire.[52] Again, the evangelists allow various apparent discrepancies to exist between their several gospels (even though these discrepancies can be resolved). This is understandable on the assumption that they are writing history.

All this indicates the existence of *an irreducible basis of fact*, recorded by eye-witnesses, and transmitted by a tradition which is treated as absolutely inviolable. If the 'facts' had been invented or enhanced, then an attempt would have been made to render the initial preaching credible by putting together a single version of it, smaller details included.

On the other hand, if the critical school and especially the modernists were correct, and the evangelists had transformed the historical facts by means of their faith, then they would have said too little. They do not include things which would have enabled the new Church to resolve the problems that confronted it: should Christians continue to observe the law

---

buried, and that he rose again the third day, according to the scriptures: and that he was seen by Cephas; and after that by the eleven" (1 Cor. 15:3–5).
52 We can note that the synoptic gospels, which were written first, do not even take the trouble to undo the bad impression this episode creates by mentioning Jesus's forgiveness of Peter, recorded later by John.

of Moses; should they preach to the pagans; should converts be circumcised? These were disputes that almost put a halt to the spread of Christianity in the early years, and even threatened its existence. "If the teaching [of the gospels] was invented by a community, why do they present the fictional Master as being silent about key questions?"[53] Again, how do we explain the fact that the canonical gospels say nothing about the physical appearance of Christ, the education which he received, or about much the greater part of his life? The apocryphal gospels, by contrast, speak at quite some length about these things, following thereby the example of the religious mythology of all times.

B. The mythical hypothesis: from God to man

On this view, Christianity is based not on historical events but on an ancient myth or legend, arising out of the deepest aspirations of the human race, about a god who becomes incarnate, suffers, dies, and rises again for the salvation of man. The 'faith' of believers supposedly invented a story with which to clothe this myth. This hypothesis corresponds to Hegel's way of thinking and was put forward in particular by Bultmann and Couchoud. "Dr Couchoud came to the conclusion that Jesus had never existed historically, and he supposed that in this way he was assigning to him a supra-historical existence, one that could not be undermined by any doubts."[54]

This hypothesis, however, comes up against one tremendous fact. After the palaeographic and archaeological discoveries of the 19th and 20th centuries, "no one henceforth can dispute the Gospel's perfect description of the Judaeo-Roman world [a world that disappeared in an unparalleled catastrophe] before the destruction of the temple of Jerusalem in AD 70." The hypothesis of myth would mean, absurdly, that a scrupulously authentic frame had been created for a false portrait. This would be something entirely unprecedented

---

53   Vittorio Messori, *Hypothèses sur Jésus*, p. 170.
54   J. Guitton, *Jésus*, pp. 40–41.

throughout the thousands of years during which myths have existed. A group of religious enthusiasts, spread across the whole Mediterranean, and writing at the end of the 1st and during the 2nd century, would not have had the wherewithal to produce such a remarkably precise geographical, chronological, political, cultural and linguistic description, with its overlapping of jurisdictions, its multitudes of sects (such as the Pharisees, the Herodians, and the Sadducees), the hierarchy of the Sanhedrin, the character of the scribes, and so on. After spending fifty years in the Holy Land, using the surviving evidence to examine the description of the world found in the gospel accounts, Fr Lagrange declared that everything in them stood up to scrutiny, and was consistent with secular history. Many details included in the gospels and now confirmed by archaeology could be mentioned, but I shall give only one: the discovery, by an excavation in 1888, of the pool with five porticoes near the Sheep Gate. This pool, which is mentioned by St John (Jn. 5:2) had been accorded a purely symbolical meaning by the 'mythologists', who had considered it to be certainly not historical.

The historical value of the New Testament, and the historical existence of Jesus, were continuously asserted by all until the 18th century. At that time, the philosophers of the Enlightenment, who would be succeeded by the rationalist thinkers of the 19th century, began to exaggerate the silence of the secular sources. In reply, one may point out that we know about Roman antiquity only through Tacitus and Suetonius—who are precisely the ones to mention Jesus!

Finally, if Christianity and the gospels were a myth, then the cross would be a clumsy and in fact wholly inexplicable invention, something entirely counter-productive. The pagan polemicist Celsus, who was very familiar with pagan mythology, wrote:

> So, God, having sent his son with a certain message, abandoned him to torments that were so cruel that the message died with him. And even though so much time

has gone by since then, he still hasn't paid any attention to it. Did anyone ever see such an unjust father (*tis outôs anosios patèr*)?[55]

C. Conclusion

By thinking things through, I came to the conclusion that there are only three possible positions about Jesus: that of Renan [the critical hypothesis], that of Hegel [the mythical hypothesis], and that of the believers. The first position makes the faith an embellishment of historical facts [Renan]; the second envisages a 'sacred history' which is spun out of pure faith [Hegel]; the third position sees a true, supernatural history [the believers].

Hence, whether we examine the gospels in themselves, or whether we consider the plausibility of the alternative theories which are put forward, we can conclude that the gospels possess an undeniable historical value.

This historicity certainly has its proper character, which corresponds to the literary genre of the gospels. For while the gospels are based on facts known to their authors, they also derive from preaching, and their purpose, under the inspiration of the Holy Spirit, is to transmit faith in Jesus, the Son of God, who became incarnate, died and rose again for our salvation:

> The four Gospels [...] faithfully hand on what Jesus Christ, while living among men, really did and taught for their eternal salvation until the day he was taken up into heaven. Indeed, after the Ascension of the Lord the Apostles *handed on* to their hearers *what he had said and done*. This they did with that clearer understanding which they enjoyed after they had been instructed by the glorious events of Christ's life and taught by the light of the Spirit of truth. The sacred authors wrote the four Gospels, *selecting* some things from the many which had been handed on by word of mouth or in writing, reducing some of them to *a synthesis*, *explaining* some things in view of the situation of their churches, and

---

55 Quoted by Origen, *Contra Celsum*, 8.41.

preserving *the form of proclamation* but always in such fashion that they told us *the honest truth about Jesus*.[56]

However, a Christian would think it silly to say that the historical value of the gospels is lessened or destroyed by their supernatural purpose, or by their inspiration by the Holy Spirit, or by the circumstances in which they came to be written. He knows that far from separating us from reality, faith allows our minds to enter into it more deeply. But even an honest man who has not yet received the grace of faith will not refuse to recognise the gospels as documents which show all the signs of being reliable witnesses, provided that he does not suffer from a rationalist prejudice, itself not susceptible of proof, against the supernatural in general and against miracles in particular. If his heart is guided by the love of truth, his enquiry will lead him to see the rational credibility of the gospels. He will come to recognise that the only coherent solution to the 'riddle' posed by Jesus's life is the one put forward by Christians: the gospels tell a true story. He will find himself then in the presence of a mystery; but grace can help him to yield himself freely to the light of faith. Only thus will he cross the threshold of the mystery of Christ.

---

[56] Vatican II, *Dei verbum* 19 (italics added); cf. CCC 126.

CHAPTER 2

Is Jesus the Messiah foretold by the prophets?

SECTION I

Prophecy and the expectation of a messianic Saviour

I. PROPHECY

   A. *The notion of prophecy*

What is a prophet? Historically, it is someone who makes known to men what God has supernaturally revealed to him and charged him to transmit. "God, who, at sundry times and in diverse manners, spoke in times past to the fathers by the prophets, last of all, in these days hath spoken to us by his Son, whom he hath appointed heir of all things, by whom also he made the world" (Heb. 1:1–2). In this broad sense, prophecy is the same thing as divine revelation.

But the term prophecy has also a more precise sense, which we find in a well-known passage of St Paul to the Corinthians. In this sense, it is a charism listed alongside other charisms such as the discernment of spirits or the power to work miracles:

> And the manifestation of the Spirit is given to every man unto profit. To one indeed, by the Spirit, is given the word of wisdom: and to another, the word of knowledge, according to the same Spirit; to another, faith in the same spirit; to another, the grace of healing in one Spirit; to another, the working of miracles; to another, prophecy; to another, the discerning of spirits; to another, diverse kinds of tongues; to another, interpretation of speeches. But all these things one and the same Spirit worketh, dividing to every one according as he will (1 Cor. 12:7–11).

In this strict sense, prophecy is the infallible prediction of a future event which is not necessary but rather entirely contingent, and which can be known with certitude only by means of a supernatural light. These properties distinguish true prophecy from counterfeits. Thus, prophecy is an infallible prediction, not a human conjecture, however shrewd or well-founded. Nor is it diabolic divination, which, like human conjectures, attains at most a probable knowledge of the future. Again, the future event which prophecy makes known is something which is not necessary. A man who announces that the sun will rise tomorrow morning is not a prophet, since this event will take place in the natural course of things, unless some cosmic cataclysm happens during the night or the end of the world arrives. Prophecy thus declares something which is truly contingent, for example, something that depends on the exercise of human freedom. If a given man plays sport, is in good health, and has no family history of disease, then to foresee that he will live a long time does not surpass the normal powers of human intelligence, or indeed those of an insurance company.

Prophecy is a 'charism', that is, a grace which is given not directly to sanctify the one who receives it, but for some useful purpose, normally for the benefit of others but sometimes for his own:

> While grace is ordained to lead men to God, this takes place in a certain order, so that some are led to God by others. And thus there is a twofold grace: one whereby man himself is united to God, and this is called sanctifying grace; the other, whereby one man cooperates in leading another man back to God, and this gift is called gratuitous grace, since it is bestowed on a man beyond the capability of nature, and beyond the merit of the person. But since it is bestowed on a man, not to justify him but so that he may cooperate in the justification of another, it is not called sanctifying grace. And it is of this that the Apostle says: "The manifestation of the Spirit is given to every man unto utility" (1 Cor. 12:7), that is, of others.[1]

---

[1] St Thomas Aquinas, *Summa Theologiae* [hereafter STh] 1a 2ae 111, 1.

The grace of prophecy takes different forms. A true prophet may know the precise moment when what he foretells will come to pass. This certainly seems to have been the case with Daniel, in his famous prophecy of the "seventy weeks of years" that would elapse between the edict to re-build Jerusalem and the coming of Christ (Dan. 9:24–27). Quite often, however, the prophet does not know when what he foretells will take place.

Again, the prophet may have certainty about the divine origin of his prophetic revelation, as Abraham when he prepared himself to sacrifice Isaac; or he may be unaware of it, as when Joseph told his brothers about his dreams.

Finally, there are cases when the prophet does not even know the real meaning of the event which he predicts, as when Caiaphas foretold the death of Christ "for the salvation of the people".[2]

B. Probative value of prophecy

The proof of Christianity by prophecies is something striking. An event that has been announced by a prophecy, once it is known to have occurred, has the nature of an 'enduring miracle'. Pascal considered this the most convincing form of proof:

> In order that men might believe in the Messiah, it was necessary that prophecies should have been made about him beforehand, and that these prophecies should have been given by people who were not open to suspicion — whose dedication, faithfulness and zeal were exceptional, and known to all the world.
>
> *The prophecies are the greatest of the proofs of Jesus Christ.* They are also that for which God made most

---

2 "But one of them, named Caiphas, being the high priest that year, said to them: You know nothing. Neither do you consider that it is expedient for you that one man should die for the people, and that the whole nation perish not. And this he spoke not of himself: but being the high priest of that year, he prophesied that Jesus should die for the nation; and not only for the nation, but to gather together in one the children of God, that were dispersed" (Jn. 11: 49–52).

provision: for the event which fulfilled them is a miracle that endures from the birth of the Church until the end. God raised up prophets for sixteen hundred years, and for the next four hundred years, he dispersed all these prophecies, along with the Jews who possessed them, to every place on earth.[3]

How can we ascertain that a prophecy has been fulfilled? One must carefully establish three things: that a certain prediction of a contingent future event was made; that a certain event has taken place; and that these two things agree. Only God, who exists outside the course of time, can know future contingents with certainty, especially those which depend on human freedom and which are therefore independent of natural causal conjunction. *A fortiori*, only God can know that which depends entirely on his own divine freedom, such as the working of a miracle, as we shall see in a later chapter.

Therefore, if a prophecy was really made and has been truly fulfilled, we have an absolutely certain sign of divine intervention. Yet here we must be careful. Certainly, unlike the horoscopes which we can buy with our newspapers, and unlike the utterances of false seers, a prophecy is never *ambiguous*, in the sense that it could be made to match more or less anything which happens. However, it does belong to a particular literary genre, that of the divine oracle, of which the fullest form is the apocalyptic vision. At the moment when a prophecy is delivered, it is generally cloaked in obscurity: we learn that something important for salvation is going to happen (for example, the coming of a saviour), and we perceive its general purport (deliverance from evil), but we do not grasp its precise nature, and still less the circumstances in which it will be realised.

It is enough that a prophecy should give us a presage of some great event and become clearer when the event itself takes place. For example, Christ's great apocalyptic discourse

---

3 Blaise Pascal, *Pensées*, nn. 571 and 706. Here and elsewhere I quote from the Brunschvicg edition.

(Matt. 24:1–31) dealt with several series of events. It enabled the Christians to flee Jerusalem when the Jewish war broke out, since it clearly prophesied the destruction of the city. On the other hand, we continue to await the end of the world, also mentioned in this prophecy, and we do not yet see the precise manner in which this will come to pass.

On the subject of prophecy, it is noteworthy that Christianity is the only religion whose 'founding charter' is contained in the holy books of 'another' religion. Hence Pascal spoke of the wonder which he experienced when reflecting on the Jewish people:

> They maintain that they are the only people in the world to whom God has revealed his mysteries; that all men are corrupt and blameworthy in God's sight; that they have all been left to their own thoughts and their own devices, and that this is why they so strangely go astray, and why both their religions and their other customs are forever changing, and they do not remain consistent in their behaviour; but that God will not leave the other peoples forever in darkness, that he will come to deliver all men; that they themselves exist in the world for the purpose of making this fact known to mankind, having been created expressly to be the forerunners and heralds of this great event, and to call all peoples to come together to await this liberator. I am full of wonder in thinking of this people; they seem to me a subject well worthy of reflection.
>
> [...] They are sincere, even when this turns to their discredit, and ready to die for what they say; there is no precedent for this in the world's history, and no explanation for it in nature.[4]

C. *The pedagogical value of prophecy*

We are considering the claim that prophecy proves the divine revelation of the Old and New Testament. We find, here, a striking idea: the true God declares what is to take place in the history of the world, from its creation out of

---

4 Pascal, *Pensées*, nn. 619 and 630.

nothing until the end of time. He sketches, as if with a few strokes, the whole history of man, as regards the 'economy of salvation'. God's revelation of himself is different in at least one important respect from other ancient cosmogonies, whether Assyro-Babylonian, Persian or Greek. In all of those cosmogonies, the history of the world overlaps with the history of the gods and of mankind. All of them are mingled together: inanimate objects, animals, stars, humanity and divinity are all seen as parts of one, eternal universe.

The biblical revelation is different. It presents God as 'He who is' (Ex. 3:14), and as having a 'duration' that transcends human history and all created time. Prophecy instructs us that the true God gives a meaning to all human history, whereas the old cosmogonies tend to evoke despair by portraying a cyclical universe in which events eternally recur.

We can also note that while the biblical prophecies are fulfilled with certainty, this usually happens in a surprising manner. This is because God always does more than man expects, since God has in view our true happiness, which is eternal and supernatural. He alone knows the circumstances in which this happiness is to be realised, and although this realisation will not ignore our natural desires, these desires are subordinated to something higher. Thus, the 'Kingdom of God' which was announced by the Jewish prophets turned out to be something universal and eternal, and much greater than the national and temporal kingship for which a large part of the Jewish people was waiting.

> If it is true that to those who seek first the kingdom of God and his justice, the rest is given in addition, then we should believe that the prophetic promises about the spiritual blessings to be poured out in the messianic age exemplify this same principle. Thus the promises also announce temporal achievements, as the natural though partly conditional consequence of the spiritual blessings; they announce this to the extent at least that such achievements are compatible with, and not contrary to, the painful necessities of our life as pilgrims. [...]

Is Jesus the Messiah foretold by the prophets?

The temporal goods which always accompany Christianity, to the extent that it is accepted, are goods of the first category [higher and purer goods, such as natural morality, the law of nations, the knowledge of the spirituality of the soul, worthwhile work, the dignity of the family and of political life], not the temporal goods of the second category [lower and more material ones, such as wealth and technological advances], which are given indifferently to the good and to the wicked (Mt. 5:45).[5]

The great St Augustine of Hippo put it well: "In the Old Testament, the New Testament lies hidden, while in the New Testament, the Old is made clear *(in veteri testamento est occultatio novi, in novo testamento est manifestatio veteris)*".[6]

II. THE EXPECTATION OF A MESSIANIC SAVIOUR

A. Messianic prophecies in the Old Testament

From the first chapters of Genesis until the last of the prophets, we find a continuous series of predictions of the coming of a Saviour of the human race. He is described as having the divine anointing, or being 'the Anointed one of God'; being, in Hebrew, the 'Messiah', and in Greek, 'Christ'. There are so many texts that it is impossible to list them all within the limits of this book. I shall simply mention some of the principal prophecies, in particular those which either concern the genealogy of the Messiah or which sketch a portrait of the Saviour whom they announce.

1. THE GENEALOGY OF THE MESSIAH. The ancestry of the Saviour is clearly expressed in the Bible. He will be a descendant of the woman: "I shall put enmity between you and the woman, between your seed and hers. He will crush your head, and you will lie in wait for his heel" (Gen. 3:15). He will be of the line of Abraham: "I will bless thee, and I will multiply thy seed as the stars of heaven, and as the sand

---

5 Charles Journet, *Destinées d'Israël, À propos du salut par les Juifs*, Egloff, Paris, 1945, 'L'équivoque des prophéties', pp. 366–72.
6 St Augustine, *De catechizandis rudibus*, 4.8; cf. *Quæstiones in heptateuchum*, II.73; *In Ps.* 105, n.36; *De baptisma contra donatistas*.

that is by the sea shore: thy seed shall possess the gates of their enemies. And in thy seed shall all the nations of the earth be blessed, because thou hast obeyed my voice" (Gen. 22:17–18). He will descend from Isaac: "I will multiply thy seed like the stars of heaven: and I will give to thy posterity all these countries: and in thy seed shall all the nations of the earth be blessed" (Gen. 26:4). He will be of the line of Jacob: "Thy seed shall be as the dust of the earth: thou shalt spread abroad to the west, and to the east, and to the north, and to the south: and in thee and thy seed all the tribes of the earth shall be blessed" (Gen. 28:14).

Among the sons of Jacob, he will come from Judah: "The sceptre shall not be taken away from Juda, nor a ruler from his thigh, till he come that is to be sent, and he shall be the expectation of nations" (Gen. 49:10). Finally, he will be a son of David: "The Lord foretelleth to thee, that the Lord will make thee a house. And when thy days shall be fulfilled, and thou shalt sleep with thy fathers, I will raise up thy seed after thee, which shall proceed out of thy bowels [...] Thy house shall be faithful, and thy kingdom for ever before thy face, and thy throne shall be firm for ever" (2 Sam. 7:11–12, 16).

2. AN "IDENTIKIT PICTURE" OF THE SAVIOUR. According to the prophecies, what are the main characteristics of the messianic Saviour? There are three, which it is not easy to harmonise: this explains why many of the Jews fell into error.[7] The Messiah will be a king; he will be a servant who suffers and is then raised up; and he will be a being possessed of a mysterious transcendence.

The Messiah will be a king. This is the most evident of the attributes of the Messiah, and all the Jews were in agreement about it. It is plain from Jacob's prophecy about Judah, quoted

---

[7] Cf. Matt. 22:41–46: "The Pharisees being gathered together, Jesus asked them, saying: What think you of Christ? Whose son is he? They say to him: David's. He saith to them: How then doth David in spirit call him Lord, saying: The Lord said to my Lord, Sit on my right hand, until I make thy enemies thy footstool? If David then call him Lord, how is he his son?"

Is Jesus the Messiah foretold by the prophets?

above (Gen. 49:10). It is present in the famous oracle which the pagan seer Balaam is forced by divine inspiration to announce: "I shall see him, but not now: I shall behold him, but not near. A star shall rise out of Jacob and a sceptre shall spring up from Israel" (Num. 24:17). We find it again in the prophecy of Nathan: "Thy house shall be faithful, and thy kingdom for ever before thy face, and thy throne shall be firm for ever" (2 Sam. 7:16). The royal character of the Messiah is also magnificently revealed by the psalms, in poetic fashion: "I am appointed king by him over Sion his holy mountain, preaching his commandment. The Lord hath said to me: Thou art my son, this day have I begotten thee. Ask of me, and I will give thee the Gentiles for thy inheritance, and the utmost parts of the earth for thy possession" (Ps. 2:6–8); "Thy throne, O God, is for ever and ever: the sceptre of thy kingdom is a sceptre of uprightness. Thou hast loved justice, and hated iniquity: therefore God, thy God, hath anointed thee with the oil of gladness above thy fellows" (Ps. 45 [44]: 7–8).[8]

The Messiah, however, will be also a person who suffers and is then raised up.[9] The extraordinarily powerful "Canticles of the Suffering Servant" in Isaiah demonstrate this. Here is the most characteristic passage:

> Who hath believed our report? and to whom is the arm of the Lord revealed? And he shall grow up as a tender plant before him, and as a root out of a thirsty ground: there is no beauty in him, nor comeliness: and we have seen him, and there was no sightliness, that we should be desirous of him: Despised, and the most abject of men, a man of sorrows, and acquainted with infirmity: and his look was as it were hidden and despised, whereupon we esteemed him not. Surely he hath borne our infirmities and carried our sorrows: and we have thought him as

---

8   Cf. Ps. 72 [71]: 1–17 and 110 [109]: 1–4.
9   This emerges from an objective study of the texts. At the time of Jesus, however, the messianic hopes of Israel were unable to combine these two properties in a single person. Cf. M. J. Lagrange OP, *Le messianisme chez les Juifs au temps de Jésus (150 av. J.-C. à 200 ap. J.-C.)*, Paris, Librairie Victor Lecoffre, J. Gabalda et Cie, 1909, pp. 236–251.

it were a leper, and as one struck by God and afflicted. But he was wounded for our iniquities, he was bruised for our sins: the chastisement of our peace was upon him, and by his bruises we are healed. [...]

The Lord hath laid on him the iniquity of us all. He was offered because it was his own will, and he opened not his mouth: he shall be led as a sheep to the slaughter, and shall be dumb as a lamb before his shearer, and he shall not open his mouth. He was taken away from distress, and from judgment: who shall declare his generation? because he is cut off out of the land of the living: for the wickedness of my people have I struck him. And he shall give the ungodly for his burial, and the rich for his death: because he hath done no iniquity, neither was there deceit in his mouth. And the Lord was pleased to bruise him in infirmity: if he shall lay down his life for sin, he shall see a long-lived seed, and the will of the Lord shall be prosperous in his hand. Because his soul hath laboured, he shall see and be filled: by his knowledge shall this my just servant justify many, and he shall bear their iniquities. Therefore will I distribute to him very many, and he shall divide the spoils of the strong, because he hath delivered his soul unto death, and was reputed with the wicked: and he hath borne the sins of many, and hath prayed for the transgressors (Is. 53:1–12).

We should note that this Servant is clearly distinct from the people for whom he is suffering: "He hath borne our infirmities and carried our sorrows". Also, this 'tender plant' is a descendant of Jesse, the father of David: "There shall come forth a rod out of the root of Jesse, and a flower shall rise up out of his root" (Is. 11:1).

The prophet Zechariah also speaks of the contrasting characteristics of the promised Saviour, as king who is both victorious and humble (cf. Zech. 9:9–10). He is One who is both pierced through, and yet the source of grace (cf. Zech. 12:9–13:1). He is a shepherd who is struck (Zech. 13:7), but who will be the cause of salvation for his people: "He shall call on my name, and I will hear him. I will say: Thou art my people: and he shall say: The Lord is my God" (Zech. 13:9).

Finally, the most mysterious aspect of the Messiah who is to sit on the throne of David is that *he will be a being to whom the attributes of divine transcendence are applied.* This is declared by the prophets Isaiah and Daniel. "For a child is born to us, and a son is given to us, and the government is upon his shoulder: and his name shall be called, Wonderful, Counsellor, God the Mighty, the Father of the world to come, the Prince of Peace. His empire shall be multiplied, and there shall be no end of peace: he shall sit upon the throne of David, and upon his kingdom; to establish it and strengthen it with judgment and with justice" (Is. 9:6–7). "I beheld therefore in the vision of the night, and lo, one like the son of man came with the clouds of heaven, and he came even to the Ancient of days: and they presented him before him. And he gave him power, and glory, and a kingdom: and all peoples, tribes and tongues shall serve him: his power is an everlasting power that shall not be taken away: and his kingdom that shall not be destroyed" (Dan. 7:13–14).

B. *The times are fulfilled*

The 'Christian era' began at the moment when the expectation of the coming of the Messiah was at its height. The prophecy of Jacob mentioned above (Gen. 49:10) foretold that the end of the Jews' temporal power would coincide with the Messiah's appearance. But Herod the Great, a tyrant who magnificently adorned the temple but who also made himself guilty of countless atrocities, including the massacre of the innocents, was the last Jewish king.

> At his death, the territory of Israel is dismembered; all real authority passes to the Roman governors, and any appearance of autonomy is gone. The Jews will never again be the masters in the land of their fathers, until 14th May, 1948, when the British mandate in Palestine came to an end.[10]

---

10 Vittorio Messsori, *Hypothèses sur Jésus*, p. 82.

Hence, at the moment of Jesus's passion, the high priests can cry out: "We have no king but Caesar!" (Jn. 19:15).

A famous prophecy of Daniel, called "the prophecy of the seventy weeks of years", explains why expectations of the Messiah were so lively at this time. "Seventy weeks are shortened upon thy people, and upon thy holy city, that transgression may be finished, and sin may have an end, and iniquity may be abolished; and everlasting justice may be brought; and vision and prophecy may be fulfilled; and the saint of saints may be anointed" (Dan. 9:24). This very precise Messianic time-line, which is the only prophecy of its kind in the Old Testament, begins from the moment of "the going forth of the word, to build up Jerusalem again" (Dan. 9:25). Depending on whether one identifies this order to re-build with a decree of Cyrus in 538 BC, or with a decree of Artaxerxes in 458 BC, the end-point is either 48 BC or AD 32. It is now known that the calculations of the Essenes produced the date of 26 BC, which is when they withdrew into the desert to await the imminent liberation which the Messiah would bring. This explains why, at about the start of the Christian era, the Jews considered that the Messianic age was close. St Luke in his gospel allows us to glimpse the state of mind of the Jewish people, eagerly looking to the fulfilment of the prophecies as John the Baptist was preaching: "As the people were of opinion, and all were thinking in their hearts of John, that perhaps he might be the Christ" (Lk. 3:15).

When Peter and John come to be judged by the Sanhedrin, Rabbi Gamaliel makes reference to certain 'Messiahs' who had recently come to prominence and who had all failed:

> Ye men of Israel, take heed to yourselves what you intend to do, as touching these men. For before these days rose up Theodas, affirming himself to be somebody, to whom a number of men, about four hundred, joined themselves: who was slain; and all that believed him were scattered, and brought to nothing. After this man, rose up Judas of Galilee, in the days of the enrolling, and

drew away the people after him: he also perished; and all, even as many as consented to him, were dispersed. And now, therefore, I say to you, refrain from these men, and let them alone; for if this council or this work be of men, it will come to nought; but if it be of God, you cannot overthrow it, lest perhaps you be found even to fight against God (Acts 5:35–39).

Still other 'Messiahs' arose at the time of the two great Jewish revolts, in AD 66–70 and AD 132. The Jewish author Flavius Josephus, who had a good knowledge of both Roman and Jewish society, wrote thus about the great Jewish War: "What had especially incited [the Jews] to wage war was an ambiguous prophecy, also found in the Holy Scriptures, which announced that at that time, a man of their country would obtain mastery over all things."[11]

C. The expectation of the peoples

It was not only the Jews who, around the time of Jesus Christ, were waiting for some great and liberating event. The idea that a saviour-king would come from Judaea at that time was found among the peoples of the East, and this expectation was itself known in the West. The *Stellar Calendar of Sippar*, which was only rediscovered and published in 1925, shows that the Babylonian astronomers had observed a planetary conjunction in 7 BC which occurs only every 794 years: Jupiter (the planet of rulers, according to their beliefs) and Saturn (the planet of the protectors of Israel) were in the constellation of Pisces (the sign of 'the end times'). The great astronomer Kepler made the same calculation in 1603.

Two Latin historians, writing between the end of the 1st century and the start of the 2nd, record the long-standing belief, widespread in the East, that "the rulers of the world would come from Judaea". Although these two official Roman authors suppose that the prophecy applied to Titus and Vespasian, they afford us a valuable witness to Jewish belief.

---

11 Flavius Josephus, *The Jewish War*, VI.V.4.

Not many Jews were frightened by these portents, as most of them believed in a prediction which they said was contained in the ancient books of their priests, that "the East would prevail, and that the masters of the world would come forth from Judaea".[12]

An old tradition held sway in the East from time immemorial: the Fates had foretold that certain people would come from Judaea at that time and would become the masters of the world. This prophecy really related to a Roman emperor, as events proved, but the Jews applied it to themselves. They rose up in rebellion, put their governor to death, expelled the consular legate of Syria who had come to help him, and took away his Eagle-standard.[13]

D. Conclusion

The Italian journalist Vittorio Messori spent ten years researching the origins of Christianity and finished by converting. He paints a vivid picture of the various expectations existing in the world during the last years before the birth of Jesus of Nazareth.

> The people of Israel are thinking about the end of their political independence, and remembering how Jacob had declared that the longed-for Christ would come just before "the sceptre passes from Judah".
>
> From the desert, the Essenes are calling upon others to join them, to wait with them in prayer and penance for the One who is to come: and their calculation of the date of his coming is disconcertingly accurate.
>
> The ordinary people in the Roman empire are excited. Pagans though they are, they keep their eyes on Israel with a keen interest. The populace is so stirred up that the learned historians who write Caesar's annals condescend to make a reference to it.
>
> In the plains of Mesopotamia, astronomy and astrology unite in their assertion that a Messiah will come from Judaea to rule the world, and that his reign will begin in the year which we inaccurately refer to as the seventh before Jesus Christ. [...]

---

12 Tacitus, *Histories*, 5.13.4.
13 Suetonius, *Lives of the Twelve Caesars*, 'Vespasian', IV.9–10.

Is Jesus the Messiah foretold by the prophets?

History seems therefore to offer its own enigmatic witness to the truth of the words attributed to Jesus in the gospel: "The time is fulfilled, and the kingdom of God is at hand" (Mk. 1:14).[14]

SECTION II

The fulfilment of the prophecies

IN THIS SECTION, I SHALL FIRST OF ALL SET forth the proofs in virtue of which, by using human reason alone, we can be convinced of the following statement: "The fulfilment of the prophecies of the Old Testament proves the divine mission of Jesus of Nazareth and the reliability of his testimony." Next, to support this statement, I shall show how from the beginning, Jesus and the apostles used the argument from prophecy. Finally, I shall explain the Catholic doctrine on this question.

I. THE FULFILMENT OF THE PROPHECIES IN JESUS OF NAZARETH

This part of our study divides naturally in two. Part (A) is addressed to those who profess to accept the authority of the Old Testament as the word of God. We shall see (a) that Jesus did indeed realise in his person the characteristics that had been foretold as belonging to the Messiah and (b) that none of the rival conceptions of the Messiah were ever realised, a fact which confirms our position by an argument *ad absurdum*. Part (B) will show that the unique and unforeseeable change which Jesus of Nazareth produced in the very conception of religion had been announced at least three centuries earlier in the books which the Jews considered sacred, and that this fact is a sure sign of his

---

14 V. Messori, *Hypothèses sur Jésus*, p. 94. We may note the author's careful choice of words: "History *seems* to offer its own *enigmatic* witness". The historical facts do not yield a scientific demonstration but offer a collection of signs of a prophetic kind, and which all point in one direction.

divine origin. A long extract from a talk given by a 19th century French Dominican, Henri-Dominique Lacordaire, will highlight the power of this argument, which "proves both testaments at once".

A. For those who recognise the Old Testament

(A) POSITIVE PROOF. Jesus fulfils the idea of the Messiah that was entertained by righteous people such as Zachariah, Simeon and John the Baptist. Their expectation was for a religious and long-suffering Messiah, who would inaugurate a universal, spiritual kingdom. This conception of the Messiah is evident especially in John the Baptist's preaching of repentance or *metanoia* (change of heart), and in the first two chapters of St Luke,[15] as also in the fact that Jesus is presented as "the Lamb of God who takes away the sin of the world" (Jn. 1:29). The expectation which the Samaritans had of a "Saviour of the world" who "will explain all things" (Jn. 4:25, 42) suggests the same ideal.

Jesus, in fact, fulfilled many prophecies, including those of a more detailed kind. He is born of a virgin (Is. 7:14) in Bethlehem (Mic. 5:1). He is the son of David (2 Sam. 7:11–16). He has a forerunner (Mal. 3:1). He performs countless miracles (Is. 35:5–6). He is gentle and humble (Is. 11:1–4; 42:2–3). He institutes a new sacrifice (Mal. 1:11) and a new covenant (Jer. 31:31–34). He is rejected by many (Is. 6:9–13; Ps. 118 [117]: 10–12) and undergoes redemptive sufferings for our sins (Is. 52–53). Finally, he rises again (Ps. 16 [15]:9–11), sends the Holy Spirit (Joel 3:1–5) and his religion spreads throughout the world (Is. 60:1–22). While all these fulfilments of prophecy are striking, what is particularly convincing is the way in which they all fit together, and are united around his passion and resurrection. This shows that he accomplished

---

[15] See the canticle of Zechariah, the *Benedictus* (Lk. 1:68–79); the song of the angels at Christ's birth (Lk. 2:14); the canticle of Simeon, the *Nunc dimittis* (Lk. 2:29–32); and the description of the prophetess Anna (Lk. 2:38). All these Scriptural passages speak of a Messiah who will bring holiness, justice, mercy, enlightenment, peace and deliverance.

the messianic mission in a way that was quite different from the 'carnal' ideas about the Messiah which were widespread at the time. Messori writes:

> What we need to consider is not just whether, in any given case, an event of Jesus's life really fulfils one of the ancient prophecies about the Messiah, even though this also is important. Before concerning ourselves with the details, we should consider the fact that the schema of 'passion-death-resurrection' could not have been simply copied from the prophecies as they were then understood, since the prophets were read at the time in quite a different way.[16]

On the other hand, the same author is mistaken in what he goes on to say: "Annas, Caiaphas, the members of the Sanhedrin, the scribes, the Pharisees and the Sadducees were all fundamentally correct from the Jewish point of view in refusing to accept this poor Galilean as the Messiah" (p. 260). Although a number of modern exegetes share this view, it is rejected by the evangelist St John, when he records these words of Jesus: "If I had not done among them the works that no other man hath done, they would not have sin; but now they have both seen and hated both me and my Father. But that the word may be fulfilled which is written in their law: They hated me without cause" (Jn. 15:24–25). The examples of Nicodemus and Joseph of Arimathea, who were members of the Sanhedrin and believed in Jesus's divine mission, show that the blindness of a large part of the Jewish establishment was not inevitable.

Jesus of Nazareth harmonised the apparently contradictory attributes which had been prophesied as belonging to the Messiah. To have thus brought prophecies which seemed incompatible into a higher unity is something striking, even astounding. Pascal put it well: "He showed, in his coming, a splendour which is all his own."

---

16   Vittorio Messori, *Il a souffert sous Ponce-Pilate. Enquête historique sur la passion et la mort de Jésus,* Paris, François-Xavier de Guibert, 1995, p. 256.

Archimedes would still be just as respected today, even if he had not been of high rank. He did not leave behind him any great military victory for mankind to contemplate: rather, he left great discoveries, and men's minds have indeed been dazzled by what he discovered.

Jesus Christ had no possessions, nor did he make known any new scientific discovery; his greatness is that of holiness. He left behind him no new invention. He never held power. He was humble, and patient, and holy; he was holy in God's sight, and terrible to the demons; he was without sin. And therefore, to the eyes of the heart, which alone can perceive wisdom, he came indeed in great splendour and magnificence.

Although Archimedes was a prince, it would have been pointless for him to have written his books of geometry in a princely style. And likewise, it would have been pointless for our Lord Jesus Christ to have come as a king in order to make manifest his holy reign. What he showed in his coming was a splendour which is all his own.[17]

(B) NEGATIVE PROOF. At the time of Jesus of Nazareth, although all the Jews were waiting for the Messiah, they differed among themselves in their ideas of what the Messiah would be like. We have a good understanding, today, of the different groups and their various opinions. Roughly speaking, there were three main views of the nature and role of the Messiah.[18]

1. A popular and this-worldly notion: he would be a temporal king who would bestow endless material blessings;

2. The rabbinic view: the Messiah would come in a glorious manner; he would observe the law, free the people from all their external enemies, and establish a national kingdom which would rule over all other peoples: this would be the 'reign of God'.

3. An eschatological and apocalyptic idea: this identified the coming of the Messiah with the end of the world and the last judgement.

---

17 Pascal, *Pensées*, 793.
18 Cf. M. Nicolau, *Sacrae Theologiae Summa*, I. *Theologia fundamentalis*, 'De revelatione christiana', BAC, Madrid, 1962, pp. 298–300.

It is obvious from history that none of these three expectations was realised. Hence, if one accepts the truth of the messianic prophecies of the Old Testament, one is logically bound to accept Jesus as the promised Messiah, as the 'Messianic Jews' do today. However, many among the Jewish people who have not accepted Christ have now wearied of looking for a Messiah who never comes. They have given up the precise and personal conception of the Messiah found in the Old Testament and replaced it with a vague idea of an abstract or 'collective' Messiah.

B. Proof by reason alone

The Old Testament included within itself a promise that the old covenant would be fulfilled and at the same surpassed by a spiritual and universal covenant. This extraordinary event was prophesied before it came to pass:

> The spirit of the Lord is upon me, because the Lord hath anointed me: he hath sent me to preach to the meek, to heal the contrite of heart, and to preach a release to the captives, and deliverance to them that are shut up. To proclaim the acceptable year of the Lord, and the day of vengeance of our God: to comfort all that mourn (Is. 61:1–2).
>
> Behold the days shall come, saith the Lord, and I will make a new covenant with the house of Israel, and with the house of Juda: not according to the covenant which I made with their fathers, in the day that I took them by the hand to bring them out of the land of Egypt: the covenant which they made void, and I had dominion over them, saith the Lord. But this shall be the covenant that I will make with the house of Israel, after those days, saith the Lord: I will give my law in their bowels, and I will write it in their heart: and I will be their God, and they shall be my people. And they shall teach no more every man his neighbour, and every man his brother, saying: Know the Lord: for all shall know me from the least of them even to the greatest, saith the Lord: for I will forgive their iniquity, and I will remember their sin no more (Jer. 31:31–34).

CHRISTIANITY IS CREDIBLE

Jesus of Nazareth brought about this change and this fulfilment. While someone might question whether a given detail in a prophecy has been realised, this constitutes a supreme fact, which cannot be denied:

> It is impossible to explain away the great religious fact of the effect which [Jesus's] holiness produced on the apostles and on the world. This effect, which was supported by his miracles, *had been predicted in advance*. The details of a story can always be skilfully arranged from motives of piety, but no mere artistic skill, however pious, could bring about the moral and religious change which Jesus caused. The confidence with which the apostles announced that the expected Messiah had come, without any of the outward signs of temporal glory which the Jews had been relying on, could not be merely the result of an ingenious interpretation of the prophecies. No: they saw, and understood what they had seen, and declared what they had understood.[19]

St Thomas Aquinas sees this religious change, prophesied in advance despite its unlikelihood, as one of the strongest arguments of credibility in favour of faith in Christ. In an inspired passage of the *Summa contra Gentiles*, he joins the argument from miracles, which we shall speak about in the next chapter, with the argument from prophecy:

> Those, however, who place their faith in this truth [of the faith] "of which the human reason has no experience" [St Gregory the Great, Homily 16.1 on the gospels] do not believe foolishly, as though "following ingenious fables" (2 Peter 2:16). For these "secrets of divine Wisdom" (Job 11:6), the divine Wisdom itself, which knows all things to the full, has deigned to reveal to men. [...] For the minds of mortal men to assent to these things is the greatest of miracles, just as it is a manifest work of divine inspiration that, spurning visible things, men should seek only what is invisible. *Now, that this has happened neither without preparation nor by chance, but as a result of the disposition of God, is clear from the fact*

---

19 M.-J. Lagrange, 'Pascal et les prophéties', *Revue Biblique*, 1906 (New series, year 3), p. 533–560 [553].

that through many pronouncements of the ancient prophets God had foretold that he would do this. The books of these prophets are held in veneration among us Christians, since they give witness to our faith.

The letter to the Hebrews refers to the manner of this: "Which," that is, human salvation, "having begun to be declared by the Lord, was confirmed to us by them that hear him: God also bearing them witness of signs, and wonders, and diverse miracles, and distributions of the Holy Spirit" (Heb. 7:3–4). This wonderful conversion of the world to the Christian faith is the clearest witness of the signs given in the past; so that it is not necessary that they should be further repeated, since they appear most clearly in their effect. For it would have been a miracle more surprising that all the others if, without any signs worthy of admiration, the world had been led by simple and humble men to believe such lofty truths, to accomplish such difficult actions, and to hope for such high things.[20]

Pascal also insists on the probative force of the messianic prophecies as fulfilled by Jesus Christ. He speaks in particular of the institution of a law which would be *primarily* not a matter of external observances, even though it would involve some such observances, but rather something written deep in man's heart, as Jeremiah had foretold:

Predictions. — It was predicted that at the time of the Messiah, he would establish a new covenant, which would make them forget the exodus from Egypt; it would place the law not in something external but in their hearts. It would cause the fear of God to be in the midst of their heart, so that it was no longer dependent on external punishments. One can hardly fail to see this as a reference to the Christian law.

It was also predicted that he would teach mankind a perfect way of life. Never has there been any man, either before or since, who has taught anything nearly so divine as that [...]

---

20 St Thomas Aquinas, *Summa contra Gentiles* [hereafter SCG], book 1, chapter 6: "That it is not weak-minded to give one's assent to matters of faith, even though they surpass reason".

> The Jews refuse him; and yet, not all of them. The saints among them receive him, while the carnal-minded do not. And so far is that from being an objection, that it tends rather to make his glory perfect. For the reason that they give for rejecting him, the only one to be found in their writings, in the Talmud and the other Rabbinical works, is that Jesus Christ did not subdue the nations with main force, *gladium tuum, potentissime.* Is that all they can say? Jesus Christ was killed, they say; he failed; he did not subdue the nations with his power; he did not bestow on us their spoils; he does not enrich us at all. Is that all they can say? It is precisely for acting thus that he should be loved! I would not want the messiah whom they dream of.[21]

Fr Marie-Joseph Lagrange was the founder of the *École Biblique* in Jerusalem and had a thorough knowledge of the ancient near East. He takes up the same argument as Aquinas and Pascal, and expresses it vividly:

> The ancient near East is far better understood today than previously, and we have discovered many similarities between Israel and other cultures, even in religious practices; yet outside Israel there is absolutely nothing which resembles the prayer and aspiration of the Jews for forgiveness, justice and holiness, a prayer which itself is guaranteed by a promise from God. Even after all the researches which have been carried out by students of comparative religion, this uniqueness of Israel remains an indubitable fact. God made this promise and he kept it: what had been prophesied came true.[22]

C. "Proving both testaments at once"

Sixty years before Fr Lagrange wrote, Fr Henri-Dominique Lacordaire spoke in the cathedral of Notre Dame in Paris to an audience made up largely of agnostics. In masterly fashion, Lacordaire developed Pascal's idea of a rational proof of the divine mission of Jesus Christ, from the Old Testament prophecies taken as a whole. Pascal had written: *"Proof of*

---

21 Blaise Pascal, *Pensées.* 729, 733, 760.
22 M.-J. Lagrange, 'Pascal et les prophéties', *Revue Biblique*, 1906, p. 555.

both testaments at once. In order to prove both at once, we need only see whether the prophecies contained in the one were fulfilled in the other."[23] Here are the most relevant passages from Lacordaire's outstanding speech.

> The Jewish people is the most noteworthy social and religious body of the period that preceded Jesus Christ, just as the Catholic Church is the most noteworthy social and religious body of the new age. And just as Jesus Christ is the 'soul' of the Catholic Church, and his life is perpetuated within her, so also he was the soul of the Jewish people, in whom he pre-existed. [...]
>
> The messianic idea comprised four elements. First of all, the Jewish people believed that the one God whom it worshipped, the Creator of all things, would become *the God of all the earth.* Next, it believed that this revolution would be brought about by a single man, called the Messiah, the Holy one, the Just one, the Saviour, the Desired of the nations. Thirdly, it believed that this man would be a Jew, of the tribe of Judah and of the house of David. Finally, it believed that this predestined man would suffer and die to accomplish the transformation which divine providence had charged him to bring about. [...]
>
> Thus, Gentlemen, it is certain that the messianic idea was the soul of the Jewish people during the two thousand years that preceded Jesus Christ. [...] It was an idea that was extraordinary both in its universal scope, and in the way in which it developed and endured down the ages. Has this idea been fulfilled? Yes: the one, Creator God of the Hebrew bible has become the God of all the earth, and even those nations which as a whole have not yet accepted him, still pay him homage in the persons of those worshippers whom providence has raised up among them. Who brought about this astonishing change? One man, Christ. And who was he? He was a Jew, of the tribe of Judah, of the house of David. How did he bring about this great social and religious revolution? By suffering and dying, as David, Isaias, and Daniel had foretold.

---

23 Blaise Pascal, *Pensées*, 642.

CHRISTIANITY IS CREDIBLE

Now, Gentlemen, I ask you: what do you make of this? We have two facts here which correspond to each other: the messianic idea and its fulfilment. These two facts are certain, and they are also vast. One of them occupied a period of two thousand years before Jesus Christ, while the other has lasted for eighteen hundred years since Jesus Christ. One of them spoke of a revolutionary change, humanly impossible to predict; the other is that very change. Jesus Christ is the beginning and the end of each of them, and he unites them. Once again, I ask you: what do you make of this? Will you try to deny it? But what exactly will you deny?

Will you deny the existence of the messianic idea? Yet it exists within the Jewish people, who are a living reality, and we come across it in their history at every turn. We find it also in the traditions of the human race as a whole, as even the most convinced sceptics expressly declare.[24] Will you deny the antiquity of the various details of the prophecies? The Jewish people, which crucified Jesus Christ and which therefore has a strong and long-standing motive to deprive him of the proofs of his divinity, tells you that its Scriptures today are the same as they were of old;[25] and, to make us the more sure of this, two hundred and fifty years before Jesus Christ, during the reign of Ptolemy Philadelphus of Egypt and at his command, the whole of the Old Testament was translated into Greek and thus came into the possession of Greeks and Romans, and of the whole civilised world.

Will you turn, then, to the other side of the question, and deny that the messianic idea has been fulfilled? Behold, the Catholic Church, the Church of your baptism. She was born from this very idea. Or is it the connexion of the two great facts that you will attempt to dispute? Then will you deny that Jesus Christ realised the messianic idea in his own person, that he was a

---

[24] Lacordaire had previously quoted some of the 18th century rationalists, including Voltaire, Volney and Boulanger.
[25] The discovery of the Dead Sea Scrolls in 1949, which included in particular a complete copy of Isaiah with a text identical to that of our modern bibles, was a striking confirmation of the fact that Scripture has remained unchanged.

Jew, that he came of the tribe of Judah, of the house of David, that he was the founder of the Catholic Church, which is built on the twin ruins of the synagogue and of idolatry? If you do so, then will either of the two interested parties agree with you, they who are nonetheless irreconcilable enemies to each other? The Jew says 'Yes, Jesus was that and he did that'. The Christian says the same.

Then will you say that the correspondence of these two great facts, the messianic ideal and the Catholic Church, and their being joined together by Jesus Christ, was a mere chance? But if there is such a thing as chance, it means a brief and fortuitous accident: chance, by definition, cannot be a long series of events. A chance does not continue for two thousand years, and then for eighteen centuries more.

Or finally, will you say that the Jewish people were ambitious and religious-minded, and that they engaged in a long conspiracy in order to make themselves seem important in the world? Really? A conspiracy lasting two thousand years, depending on a leader who had to be waited for during sixty generations, and who would not only have to be waited for so patiently, but who would also have to be finally created by human skill. [...]

Gentlemen, when God is at work, nothing can resist him. Jesus Christ's influence over the past is of even more striking dimensions than his influence during his life and beyond, divine though that is. When one is alive, after all, one possesses a certain power of action; it is possible to imagine circumstances which would provide favourable opportunities for a man of unusual genius, giving him a great sway over his contemporaries. Even after such a man had died, his friends and disciples would remain, and they would remember the life he had lived. In that sense, such a man could continue to act. But when it comes to the time that elapsed before we existed, when it comes to the past, who can influence that? The greatest man among us cannot choose his own ancestor. When we wish to propagate some teaching, do we fashion the generations that came before us, in order to make them faithful adherents of a doctrine that does not yet exist? [...] No: the past is an inaccessible land. It is a place where not even God can act, except insofar as he prepares the way for something which is to come. If Jesus Christ had come into the world as we do, at a chance moment between past and future; if he had not by his providence pre-existed the moment of his coming, then he would in vain have looked to the annals of by-gone days and shown that they spoke of him for twenty centuries before his birth.[26]

II. CONFIRMATION: THE USE OF THE ARGUMENT FROM PROPHECY BY JESUS AND THE APOSTLES

A. Jesus

Even a rather superficial reading of the gospels shows that Jesus of Nazareth presented himself as fulfilling the prophecies of the Old Testament. At the beginning of his public ministry, in the synagogue at Nazareth, he applies to himself the prophecy of Isaiah mentioned above, concerning the fullness of the Spirit which would rest upon the Messiah (Is. 61:1–2). Having rolled up the scroll, he tells his astonished hearers: "Today this Scripture is fulfilled in your hearing" Lk. 4:16–21). To the messengers of John the Baptist, he makes clear, in a way that would have been impossible for anyone who knew the Scriptures to misunderstand, that he is indeed the Messiah (Lk. 7:18–23), citing other passages from Isaiah, which predict the very miracles that he has worked in their presence; at the same time, he tells them that these miracles exist for the sake of the preaching of the gospel (Is. 29:18ff; 26:19; 35:5–6; 61:1). We also see here that he is fully aware that his contemporaries will find it difficult to accept him as the Messiah: "Blessed is he who is not scandalised at me" (Lk. 7:23). Again, Jesus explicitly tells the Samaritan woman at Jacob's well that he is the Messiah, the Christ who was foretold: "I am he who speak with you" (Jn. 4:26). In his disputation with the Pharisees after the cure of the sick man at the Sheep pool, Jesus appeals to the witness of the prophets about himself: "Search

---

26 Henri-Dominique Lacordaire, 41st Conference of Notre Dame, given in 1846, and published as *De la préexistence de Jésus-Christ*, Poussielgue, 1906, vol. 3, pp. 121, 135, 145–50.

the scriptures, for you think in them to have life everlasting; and the same are they that give testimony of me. And you will not come to me that you may have life" (Jn. 5:39–40).

Finally, after his passion and resurrection, Jesus gives to his disciples a new kind of catechesis, in which he shows them that the events which have just occurred fulfil the contrasting elements in the prophecies, which had spoken of a Messiah who would be both humbled and exalted. "Beginning at Moses and all the prophets, he expounded to them in all the scriptures, the things that were concerning him. [...] He said to them: These are the words which I spoke to you, while I was yet with you, that all things must needs be fulfilled, which are written in the law of Moses, and in the prophets, and in the psalms, concerning me. Then he opened their understanding, that they might understand the scriptures" (Lk. 24:27, 44–45).

Jesus had to insist especially upon the spiritual and 'interior' aspect of the messianic kingdom, since the people found this hard to accept, given the hopes of temporal liberation and dominion which they cherished.[27] Nevertheless, he also made the triumphant character of his messianic kingship a part of his preaching, not least when he addressed the Sanhedrin on one solemn occasion. When explicitly and publicly asked about his messiahship by the nation's highest religious dignitary, Jesus replied affirmatively. "But Jesus held his peace. And the high priest said to him: I adjure thee by the living God, that thou tell us if thou be the Christ the Son of God. Jesus saith to him: Thou hast said it. Nevertheless I say to you, hereafter you shall see the Son of man sitting on the right hand of the power of God, and coming in the clouds of heaven" (Mt. 26:63–64). By this reference to the seventh chapter of Daniel, Jesus is asserting that in himself are to be found *all* the attributes which the prophets had said would belong to the Messiah — yet not in the way that many people were expecting.

---

27 Cf. CCC 469, quoted below.

B. The apostles

A person need only read through the first gospel, St Matthew's, to see how frequently arguments from prophecy are used to support the mission of Jesus of Nazareth. We frequently find the phrase, "this happened to fulfil what was said by the prophet..."[28]

Likewise, in the gospel of St John, the fact that Jesus is the Messiah is affirmed from the beginning. "Philip findeth Nathanael, and saith to him: We have found him of whom Moses in the law, and the prophets did write, Jesus the son of Joseph of Nazareth" (Jn. 1:45). The evangelist speaks in several places of the fulfilment of the Scriptures, both in regard to Christ's resurrection (Jn. 2:2; 20:9), and also to point out how certain details of the Passion had been foretold, including the dividing of Jesus's clothes by the soldiers after the crucifixion (Jn. 19:24), Jesus's thirst on the Cross and the vinegar which was offered to him (Jn. 19:28), and the fact that no bone of Jesus was broken (Jn. 20:9).

The prince of the apostles speaks in a similar way. For St Peter, the Transfiguration was a marvellous proof of how the prophecies were fulfilled in Jesus: "We have the prophetic word made more sure" (2 Pet. 1:19). In his very first speech to the Jews, on the day of Pentecost, Peter quotes from a psalm of David in order to prove that the resurrection of Jesus of Nazareth, to which the apostles were witnesses, was foretold by the prophets: "Whereas therefore he was a prophet, and knew that God hath sworn to him with an oath, that of the fruit of his loins one should sit upon his throne. Foreseeing this, he spoke of the resurrection of Christ. For neither was he left in hell, neither did his flesh see corruption. This Jesus hath God raised again, whereof all we are witnesses" (Acts 2:30–32). Again, speaking to the centurion Cornelius, Peter explains that the prophets foretold that salvation would come through faith in Christ: "To him all the prophets give

---

28 Cf. Matt. 1:22; 2:5, 15, 17, 23; 3:3; 4:14; 8:17; 12:17; 13:35; 21:4; 26:56; 27:9, 35

testimony, that by his name all receive remission of sins, who believe in him" (Acts 10:43).

St Paul, the teacher of the nations, declares that Jesus Christ and his gospel were "promised by the prophets" (Rom. 1:2; 16:25). He makes abundant use of arguments from prophecy when speaking to the Jews, during his stay in Rome: "He expounded, testifying the kingdom of God, and persuading them concerning Jesus, out of the law of Moses and the prophets" (Acts 28:23).

III. CATHOLIC TEACHING

Not only have the Fathers and doctors of the Church always made use of arguments from prophecy, but their importance has also been emphasised by the magisterium. In 1442, the council of Florence declared concerning our Lord Jesus Christ that "his future coming was foretold by all the holy sacrifices, sacraments and ceremonies of the Old Testament".[29] In 1870, the 1st Vatican Council, in a dogmatic constitution treating of the nature of faith and its relationship with reason, spoke of the 'motives of credibility' which underlie the supernatural act of faith. Among the most important of these motives, it mentions the fulfilment by Jesus of Nazareth of the messianic prophecies:

> Nevertheless, in order that the obedience of our faith might be in harmony with reason, God willed that to the interior help of the Holy Spirit there should be joined exterior proofs of his revelation; to wit, divine facts, and *especially miracles and prophecies* (*in primis miracula et prophetias*), which, as they manifestly display the omnipotence and infinite knowledge of God, are *most certain proofs of his divine revelation, adapted to the intelligence of all men*. Wherefore, both *Moses and the Prophets*, and most especially, Christ our Lord himself, showed forth many and most evident miracles, and *prophesied*; and of the Apostles we read: "But they going

---

29 Bull *Cantate Domino*, Denzinger-Schönmetzer [hereafter DS] 1347. Denzinger and Schönmetzer were the editors of a well-known collection of Church documents.

forth preached everywhere, the Lord working withal, and confirming the word with signs that followed." And again, it is written: "We have the more firm *prophetical word*, whereunto you do well to attend, as to a light shining in a dark place".[30]

In the encyclical letter *Pascendi Dominici gregis*, St Pius X shows how a division between the 'Jesus of history' and the 'Jesus of faith' would do away with the probative force of the prophecies. The holy pontiff explains that the modernists reason in the following way:

> Should it be further asked whether Christ has wrought real miracles, and made real prophecies, whether He rose truly from the dead and ascended into Heaven, the answer of agnostic science will be in the negative and the answer of faith in the affirmative, and yet there will not be, on that account, any conflict between them. For it will be denied by the philosopher as a philosopher speaking to philosophers and considering Christ only in his historical reality; and it will be affirmed by the believer as a believer speaking to believers and considering the life of Christ as lived again by faith and in faith [...]. The Modernist apologists pursue their way eagerly. They grant also that certain arguments adduced in the sacred books in proof of a given doctrine, like those, for example, which are based on the prophecies, have no rational foundation to rest on. But they defend even these as artifices of preaching which are justified by life.[31]

The Second Vatican Council, in its dogmatic constitution on divine revelation, refers in passing to the argument from prophecy as an undisputed truth:

> Christ the Lord, in whom the full revelation of the supreme God is brought to completion, commissioned the Apostles to preach to all men that gospel which is the source of all saving truth and moral teaching, and to impart to them heavenly gifts. This gospel had

---

30   First Vatican Council, Dogmatic constitution *Dei Filius*, ch. 3 'On Faith', DS 3009.
31   *Pascendi Dominici gregis*, 16, 36.

been promised in former times through the prophets, and Christ himself had fulfilled it and promulgated it with his lips.[32]

The *Catechism of the Catholic Church*, published in 1992, is very explicit about the fact that Jesus is the promised Messiah. It shows that he presented himself as such, although he took great care to correct an excessively temporal understanding of the title:

> The word 'Christ' comes from the Greek translation of the Hebrew 'Messiah', which means 'anointed'. It became the name proper to Jesus only because he accomplished perfectly the divine mission that 'Christ' signifies. [...] It was necessary that the Messiah be anointed by the Spirit of the Lord at once as king and priest and also as prophet. Jesus fulfilled the messianic hope of Israel in his threefold office of priest, prophet and king. [...] Many Jews and even certain Gentiles who shared their hope recognized in Jesus the fundamental attributes of the messianic 'Son of David', promised by God to Israel. Jesus accepted his rightful title of Messiah, though with some reserve because it was understood by some of his contemporaries in too human a sense, as essentially political.
>
> Jesus accepted Peter's profession of faith, which acknowledged him to be the Messiah, by announcing the imminent Passion of the Son of Man. He unveiled the authentic content of his messianic kingship both in the transcendent identity of the Son of Man "who came down from heaven" (Jn. 3:13), and in his redemptive mission as the suffering Servant: "The Son of Man came not to be served but to serve, and to give his life as a ransom for many (Matt. 20:28)".[33]

Finally, St John Paul II also mentioned the fulfilment of the messianic prophecies as a truth of which the Church is in peaceful possession, for example in his encyclical on mercy:

> By becoming the incarnation of the love that is manifested with a particular force toward the suffering, the

---

32   Second Vatican Council, Dogmatic constitution *Dei verbum*, 7.
33   CCC 436, 439–40.

unfortunate and sinners, Christ, accomplishing the messianic prophecies, makes present and thus more fully reveals the Father, who is God "rich in mercy".[34]

---

[34] Encyclical letter *Dives in misericordia*, 30th November, 1980, para. 3.

CHAPTER 3

Do the miracles of Christ prove his divinity?

SECTION I

Miracles

IN THE FIRST SECTION OF THIS CHAPTER, I shall explain the notion of a miracle. After that, I shall consider whether miracles are possible. Finally, I shall examine the possibility of recognising a miracle by means of reason alone.

I. THE CONCEPT OF A MIRACLE[1]

By its etymology, a miracle means something *wonderful*. It is something which causes admiration or surprise because it is unusual and its cause is hidden:

> The word miracle is derived from admiration, which arises when some effect is manifest, but its cause is hidden; as when a man sees an eclipse without knowing its cause, as the Philosopher says in the beginning of the *Metaphysics* [book 1, 982 p 16]. Now the cause of some manifest effect may be known to some, but unknown to others. Therefore, a thing may be wonderful to one man, and not at all to others: as an eclipse is to a rustic, but not to an astronomer. Now a miracle is so called as producing wonder fully, since its cause is absolutely hidden from all: and this cause is God. Therefore, the things which God does outside those causes which we know, are called miracles.[2]

---

1 A valuable study on this subject is *Le miracle et la foi*, ed. Philippe-Marie Margelidon OP, Acts of the Colloquium of 21st to 22nd October 21–22 at Rocamadour (Artège-Lethielleux, 2017). The various papers given at this colloquium can "contribute to a better understanding of how and why the revelation of God as creator and as saviour in Jesus Christ is incomprehensible or perhaps even unreasonable without miracles" (p. 23).
2 St Thomas Aquinas, STh 1a 105, 7.

CHRISTIANITY IS CREDIBLE

Since we are interested in 'signs of credibility' which would enable us to accept some message as divinely revealed, we must exclude from our conception of a miracle all actions performed by angelic or demonic power, however unusual they may be. We must exclude all the extraordinary effects which these created spirits can produce in the visible world, even though such effects may well surpass the power of man and of all bodily creatures. A miracle, in our sense, requires the action of God and reveals his power and wisdom. It is a divine sign:

> In order that the obedience of our faith might be in harmony with reason, God willed that to the interior help of the Holy Spirit there should be joined exterior proofs of his revelation; to wit, *divine facts*, and especially *miracles* and prophecies, which, as they manifestly *display the omnipotence and infinite knowledge of God* (*cum Dei omnipotentiam et infinitam scientiam luculenter commonstrent*), are *most certain signs* of his divine revelation, adapted to the intelligence of all men.[3]

We may define a miracle as "an effect produced in the world by God, and beyond the power of any created nature to achieve". It is a prodigy which is produced in this universe, the spatio-temporal world of the realities that affect our senses. It is thus always an empirical event, not a teaching, however sublime. Even though a teaching is made known by empirical means, speech or writing, it is in itself a collection of propositions, which are not as such material things. Again, something which is strictly a mystery, knowable only by faith, is not called a miracle. An example of this would be transubstantiation: the presence of Christ in the Holy Eucharist under the visible appearances of bread and wine. Nor do we refer to the elements of sanctity as miraculous, for example sanctifying grace and charity, since these are realities which are not visible in themselves.

---

3 Cf. 1st Vatican Council, Dogmatic constitution *Dei Filius*, DS 3009 (italics added).

However, miracles are not only empirical events which are beyond the power of created things to accomplish. On account of the sacred and religious context in which they occur (a point to which I shall return), they produce an effect which is quite different from the amazement which a conjurer or a magician may achieve. Miracles are also something distinct from the things that we call 'fabulous', 'legendary' or 'mythical': those terms refer to events where the facts are hard to determine and admit of various interpretations. By contrast, a miracle always clearly manifests a special intervention in the world by the Author of nature. It forces the human mind to look beyond created causality, and toward a wisdom and power surpassing those of creatures. It therefore serves as a divine sign.

Thus, unusual events with a natural explanation, and chance events, while they are certainly unforeseeable — though subject to divine providence — are nevertheless not miracles. Some pious people have a tendency to see a message from God in any kind of coincidence, even one that is only slightly improbable. But a sensible Christian, while being open to the possibility of such messages, will be careful not to exaggerate. If he thinks he sees a sign, he should normally keep it to himself and not announce it to other people, unless he has received a mission from God to do so: something which needs to be determined by the help of a spiritual father and the authority of the Catholic hierarchy. Imprudence in this regard can be a stumbling-block for many Christians who are not interested in hearing about extraordinary supernatural events, and even more so for unbelievers, when people try to convince them about the truths of the faith using these kinds of argument.

> That which is above the human reason we believe only because God has revealed it. Nevertheless, there are certain likely arguments that should be brought forth in order to make divine truth known. This should be done for the training and consolation of the faithful, and not with any idea of refuting those who are adversaries. For the very inadequacy of the arguments would rather

strengthen them in their error, since they would imagine that our acceptance of the truth of faith was based on such weak arguments.[4]

For example, while providential occurrences obtained after the making of fervent petitions are certainly encouraging, since they show the power of prayer, they are not strictly miracles. The same is true of diabolic phenomena or the visible interventions of the holy angels, since such effects come within the proper power of incorporeal, created natures. As for 'ordinary' divine effects, such as the creation of souls or justification, while these do indeed manifest infinite power, and are thus proper to God alone, they do not count as signs, since they fall within the customary scope of divine action:

> Creation, and the justification of the impious, though done by God alone, are not properly speaking miracles, because they are not apt by nature to proceed from any other cause; so they do not occur in a way that is outside the order of nature, since they do not in any case belong to that order.[5]

We may say that every miracle has three essential aspects. There is:

- an ontological, transcendent aspect: it surpasses all created power;
- a significatory aspect: it is a sign of the direct intervention of God;
- a psychological aspect: it is something extraordinary.

In the bible, both in the Old Testament (cf. Ex. 7:3; Deut. 4:34; Ps. 105 [104]:27), and in the New (cf. Jn. 4:38; Acts 2:19, 22, 43; Acts 7:36), miracles are often referred to by words such as 'works of power', 'signs' and 'prodigies'. In the common biblical expression *'sèmeia kai terata'* ('signs and wonders'), the first word denotes the intervention of God, while

---

[4] St Thomas Aquinas, SCG, book 1, chapter 9: "Ipsa rationum insufficientia eos magis in suo errore confirmaret, dum aestimarent nos propter tam debiles rationes veritati fidei consentire."
[5] St Thomas Aquinas, STh 1a 105, 7 ad 1.

the second indicates something beyond the power of nature. These two aspects are the most important ones, from which derives the third aspect, that of being something exceptional: for if God frequently or habitually acted beyond the laws of nature, then not only would the natural world be deprived of its proper integrity, but so also would the Christian life, which is a life of faith. This, incidentally, gives us a fairly good idea of the credibility of the messages which certain 'seers' claim to receive every day:

> Two things may be considered in miracles. One is that which is done: this is something surpassing the power of nature, and in this respect, miracles are called 'works of power' (*virtutes*). The other thing is the purpose for which miracles are wrought, namely the manifestation of something supernatural, and in this respect, they are commonly called 'signs'. But on account of their excellence, they receive the name of 'wonder' or 'prodigy' (*portenta vel prodigia*), as showing something from afar (*procul*).[6]

A. Different kinds of miracle

We can distinguish different kinds of miracles according to the different ways in which they surpass the powers of nature. A miracle may surpass nature:

- by the 'substance' of what is done, that is, when the effect is one that can never be produced by nature, for example, the transfiguration of a glorified human body, or the creation of matter, as in the multiplication of the loaves;

- by the subject in which the thing is done, as when the effect is one that can be produced by nature, but not in this particular subject, as when sight is given to a blind man, or life to a corpse;

- by the manner in which the thing is done, when an effect is produced in a way which nature cannot match, for example, an immediate cure preceded by none of the usual treatments.

---

6   Ibid. 2a 2ae 178, 1 ad 3.

A famous miracle called 'the miracle of the re-attached leg' seems to belong to the second category. This miracle took place on 29th March 1640, by the intercession of our Lady of the Pilar. The beneficiary was Miguel Juan Pellicer, of Calanda, in the province of Aragon in Spain:

> No trace was found of the leg, which had been buried in that section of the cemetery which was set aside for amputated limbs. [...] What occurred was not an act of creation, but an astonishing work of 'repair'. The leg did not grow back; it was re-attached. Nevertheless, there must have been some minor act of creation [...] as regards those muscles, nerves, skin, tissues and blood vessels that were destroyed by the amputation and by the terrible cauterisation with a red-hot iron which followed it.[7]

We should be careful, however, to note that while a miracle of any kind is 'outside the order of nature', one cannot strictly say that it is against, or contrary to, nature. Since 'nature' is a creature of God, God can use it for ends which are higher than its usual ones:

> God is the primary agent as we showed above [SCG book 1, ch. 13], and all other things are like instruments for him. But instruments are made for the purpose of subserving the action of the principal agent, while being moved by him. Consequently, the matter and form of an instrument should be such that they are suitable for the action which the principal agent intends. This is why it is not contrary to the nature of an instrument for it to be moved by a principal agent, but, rather, is most fitting for it. Therefore, it is not contrary to nature when created things are moved in any way by God; indeed, *they were so made that they might serve him.*
>
> [...] Furthermore, all creatures are related to God as artistic products are to an artist, as is clear from what has been shown [SCG, book 2, ch. 24]. Consequently, the whole of nature is like an artifact of the divine art. But it is not contrary to the essential character of an artist if

---

7   Vittorio Messori, *Le miracle impensable*, Paris, Mame, 2000, pp. 99–100.

he should work in a different way on his product, even after he has given it its first form. Neither, then, is it against nature if God does something to natural things in a way that differs from the customary course of nature.

Hence, Augustine says: "God, the creator and founder of all natures, does nothing contrary to nature; for what the source of all measure, number and order in nature does, is natural to each thing [*Contra Faustum*, 16.3]." [8]

B. The purpose *of miracles*

What is the purpose of miracles? It is, above all, to prove the truth of some teaching. In particular, we shall see that Jesus worked miracles to show the truth of his teaching, especially concerning his messiahship and his divinity:

> Oral teaching requires confirmation so that it may be accepted, unless it be evident in itself. Now, because things that are of faith are not evident to human reason, it was necessary for some means to be provided whereby the words of the preachers of the faith might be confirmed. Now, they could not be confirmed by any rational principles in the way of *demonstration*, since the objects of faith surpass reason. So, it was necessary for the oral teaching of the preachers to be confirmed by certain *signs*, whereby it might be plainly shown that this oral teaching came from God; so, the preachers did such things as healing the sick, and the performance of other difficult deeds, which only God could do (cf. Matt. 10:8; Mk. 16:20). [9]

Whilst there can also be secondary reasons for the working of a miracle, these latter will always have some connexion to some truth of universal relevance. For example, miracles which are worked to increase someone's faith manifest the importance which the faith has for everyone. Miracles which serve to show the holiness of the one who works them manifest the truth that the Holy Spirit dwells in the souls of the just. Those which demonstrate God's compassion for a particular

---

8   St Thomas Aquinas, SCG, book 3, ch. 100.
9   Ibid, ch. 154.

person in distress draw our attention to his unchanging goodness and providence. Christ, who went about doing good, worked many miracles in order to reveal his goodness of heart (cf. Acts 10:38; Tit. 3:4), and his absolute power over creation (cf. Rom. 8:20–22; 1 Cor. 15:24). Sometimes, also, miracles serve as symbols for some mystery of faith, as the multiplication of the loaves does in regard to the Eucharist.

Miracles, then, are first of all a general sign of credibility: they show that Christ speaks the truth when he declares that he is the Messiah and the Son of God. Secondly, they are signs which direct us to further aspects of the mystery of Christ, showing us that he is holy and good, and that he has established a 'sacramental economy' of redemption.

II. MIRACLES ARE POSSIBLE

For atheists and many agnostics, the impossibility of miracles is a settled fact. Since, in their view, there is no first cause of the universe, or at least none which can be known by reason, it is a simple absurdity to speak of them.

Some rationalistic theists argue slightly differently: they admit the existence of God, but exaggerate the necessity of the laws of nature, and so they deny that God can act outside them. This opinion, however, reveals a profound misunderstanding of the very nature of divine causality, and the way in which it differs from created causality. The laws of nature, whether physical, chemical or biological, are an expression of the causal powers of created natures. God is a free and all-powerful cause, and it is on him that all these laws of nature depend. He is therefore not limited by these laws. In technical language, they are said to have a 'hypothetical necessity': assuming that God has willed that creation consist of creatures of a certain kind, these laws follow necessarily.[10]

---

[10] Developments in modern physics have also greatly undermined belief in a deterministic universe, and also therefore the absolute necessity which some rationalist scientists attributed to physical laws.

Do the miracles of Christ prove his divinity?

God can act 'outside' the natural laws which he has established for creation, by exceptional interventions which do not undermine these laws' stability. We may note here, incidentally, that Christians do serious harm to their religion if they spend a large part of their time looking for unusual phenomena, whether apparitions, locutions, prophecies or miracles, or if they let themselves be carried away by pseudo-apparitions which supposedly involve the daily occurrence of preternatural[11] events. They demolish thereby one of the main arguments which renders their own religion credible, and, no doubt unintentionally, they can also cause unbelievers to think that the Christian understanding of miracles destroys the epistemological basis of experimental science: for if preternatural events are to be found everywhere, how can we discern the fixed laws that govern the world? We do well here to heed some words of a 20th century Jesuit theologian who studied the question of miracles in depth:

A miracle is a contingent event, forming an exception to laws which possess a merely hypothetical necessity. It is produced by the intervention of a new cause, acting in an unusual way on other causes. Experience shows us how extremely rare such a thing is: there is almost no likelihood that we shall encounter a miracle in the ordinary course of life. Being something exceptional, a miracle presupposes the existence of a law or rule which can be consistently verified.[12]

Can such truly exceptional interventions by God in his creation have a purpose which is adequate to justify them? St Thomas, the 'common doctor' of the Church, considers that they can. He gives a convincing explanation of this in a chapter of the *Summa contra gentiles*, entitled "God can

---

11 The word 'preternatural' is used broadly to refer to anything that occurs outside the usual course of nature, whether this is due to the intervention of created spirits or to God. In a narrower sense, the word is used to refer only to strange events of either angelic or demonic origin.
12 Joseph de Tonquédec, *Introduction à l'étude du merveilleux et du miracle*, Paris, Beauchesne, 1923, pp. 194–95. An event is called 'contingent' (from the Latin, *contingit*, 'it happens') when it can either take place or not; if it always occurs when the cause exists, then it is called 'necessary'.

work outside the order which he has impressed upon things, by producing effects without their proximate causes". He concludes as follows:

> This argument, that God does a thing in nature in order to manifest Himself to the minds of men, should not be regarded as of slight importance. We showed above [ch. 22] that all corporeal creatures are, in a sense, ordered to intellectual nature as an end; moreover, the end of this intellectual nature is divine knowledge, as we showed above [ch. 25]. So, it is not astonishing that some change is made in corporeal substance in order to make provision for the knowing of God by intellectual nature.[13]

This fine passage opens up a magnificent perspective: the universe is created for man, while man is created to know the truth about God. We may note, again, that miracles presuppose the existence both of a first Cause and of secondary causes which have a nature which man can know. Created beings, whether bodily or spiritual, have an essence, which the human mind can grasp, at least in a general or in an analogical way.[14] We can also know, at least in general terms, how every essence is the stable principle of a certain range of operations. This is what we mean by a *nature*: the essence of a thing considered as the source of its activities, or that from which these activities are 'born'.[15] In Greek, the word for nature is *phusis*, which comes from the verb *phuo*, meaning 'to grow' or 'to grow up'. The nature is thus the cause responsible for certain effects; it is what explains their existence.

Natural reason, however, shows that beyond all the causes whose action and effects we can observe, there exists a Cause that explains their existence and their action, and faith confirms this. Although the first Cause is free of the imperfections of secondary causes, it possesses their perfections,

---

13   SCG, book 3, ch. 99.
14   For example, we grasp the essence of bees in a 'generic' way when we know them as a kind of animal—we know their 'genus', without grasping their species. We grasp the essence of an angel in an 'analogical' way, when we know that it is a non-corporeal being.
15   Hence the Latin term *natura* comes from *nascor*, 'I am born'.

especially their capacities for action, in a higher manner. It can therefore produce the effects proper to these causes without making use of them. This explains the property of 'instantaneousness', which is "one of the most common marks of a miracle", according to a modern writer who may be considered an authority on the subject:

> A miracle is a simple act of God, acting outside space and time, even though the result of his action is a state of affairs within space and time. Miracles do not disrupt natural processes but rather transcend them. The divine action does not consist in a series of observable, recordable phenomena, and hence miracles have an instantaneous character. This is something which science finds astonishing and cannot account for. This instantaneousness is a sign that divine power has been at work. A miracle is not so much 'against nature' as 'above nature'. It is a reasonable event, but it occurs according to God's reasons. For God, also, a miracle is perfectly natural, since it belongs naturally to him to create, and to re-create.[16]

The 'ontological' conditions for a miracle may thus be expressed in certain truths which are accessible to our common human understanding of the world, in particular, the distinction between the first Cause and secondary causes. Without this distinction, miracles would not be possible.[17] Consequently, as the founder of the École Biblique remarked: "It is only within monotheism that the concept of a miracle can arise, and this was in fact the situation of the evangelists".[18] Animism, by contrast, presents us with a whole multitude of causes conceived of as directly divine, or at least as preternatural:

16 René Latourelle SJ, *Miracles de Jésus et théologie du miracle*, Éditions Bellarmin-Éditions du Cerf, Montréal-Paris, 1986, p. 361.
17 Cf. Réginald Garrigou-Lagrange, *Le sens commun. La philosophie de l'être et les formules dogmatiques*, Brannay, Éditions Nunitavit, 2010 (cf. an article of Fabrice Hadjadj in *Sedes Sapientiae*, n. 138 : « Un éblouissement métaphysique : *Le sens commun* de Garrigou-Lagrange », pp. 92–103 ; and the same author's *Dieu accessible à tous. Vue d'ensemble sur les preuves de l'existence d Dieu*, Quentin Moreau, 2015 (reviewed in *Sedes Sapientiae*, n. 139, pp. 97–98).
18 Marie-Joseph Lagrange, *L'Évangile de Jésus-Christ, avec la synopse évangélique*, Paris-Perpignan, Éditions Artège-Lethielleux, 2017, p. 666.

The animists' mistake [...] lay in dividing up divine causality between different wills, or into forces which they made into gods, and whose intentions they supposed themselves able to discern. For example, they imagined that a particular god was throwing down bolts of lightning like a man shaking a spear to drive away his enemies. They had too many miracles; they had so many, in fact, that they no longer had any at all, since they lacked the very notion of ordinary, natural causes distinct from the supernatural intervention of God.[19]

Polytheism, similarly, has a variety of gods, each able to act as he wills, behind all the different forces of nature. Pantheism, finally, sees every being as an aspect of the unique divine nature. In all three cases, the idea of true, secondary causality is understood incorrectly:

The true purpose of a miracle is not to prove that God exists. Miracles presuppose the metaphysical insight which ordinary human understanding gives us, into the existence of a God who transcends every being that either has been or could be created. The purpose of miracles is to prove that God is intervening here and now by an effect which he alone can produce, in order to bear witness to some truth which man cannot know by himself, or which has been lost sight of. A miracle guarantees the truth of a message to which it is closely linked: "No one can do a miracle in my name, and soon after speak evil of me" (Mk. 9:39). People who lack the metaphysical insight in question are not in a position to know either about God or about miracles. There is no God and there are no miracles for a dog.[20]

III. A MIRACLE CAN BE RECOGNISED FROM ITS CIRCUMSTANCES

Among agnostics and rationalists, even theistic rationalists, the most popular objection to the idea of miracles is that they could not be recognised by human reason. These

---

19 Ibid.
20 Charles Journet, *Vérité de Pascal. Essai sur la valeur apologétique des Pensées*, Éditions de l'œuvre Saint-Augustin, Saint Maurice, Switzerland, 1951.

critics affirm that we do not have a precise knowledge of all natural forces, and hence that we cannot be sure that some extraordinary event truly surpasses the forces of nature. We can reply to this objection on two levels.

A. First reply: nature has its limits

On a first level, we can note that while it is true that we do not know positively all the laws of nature, we nevertheless know negatively that there are some things which created nature cannot do:

> Cases can arise where there is simply no way to postulate an unknown but natural cause. However much we may speak about the latent physical or psychological capacities of nature, and about our own ignorance, there are still certain limits which no person of sound mind will be willing to cross. We do not know all that natural forces can do, but we know some things which they cannot do. [...] If we combine hydrogen and oxygen, we will *never* produce chlorine; if we sow wheat, roses will never spring up; and likewise, a human word will never be enough by itself to calm a storm or to raise the dead. [...] Only an insane person sows wheat and thinks that a rose-bush *may* grow up, or combines oxygen and hydrogen and thinks that it *may* produce chlorine, or thinks that something he says *may* have a power over storms and over the dead.[21]

Our human reason is spontaneously aware that certain effects can be caused only by God; metaphysics confirms this. For example, only God can produce something from nothing, such as the soul, or transform one material substance into another without any intermediary accidental changes, for example changing water into wine without the long process of ripening that takes place on the vine. Consequently, if we can establish with certainty that a genuine resurrection has occurred, or that matter has been multiplied, or that an instantaneous substantial change has taken place, we

---

21 J. de Tonquédec, *Introduction à l'étude du merveilleux*... pp. 230–31.

can know that this effect must have come from God alone.

That is the first part of the reply to the objection. It has to do with what might be called the 'physical' conditions of a miracle, namely, that the effect produced surpasses natural causes and also, consequently, the fact that it is produced in an entirely free manner. The principle of causality, expressing the deterministic working of the laws of nature, can be formulated thus: "The same causes, in the same circumstances, will produce the same effects". But in the case of a miracle, the same causes will not again produce the same effects. We might say that the only thing which is predictable about miracles is that they are unpredictable.

This reply is fundamentally sound, and in addition there are cases where one can possess absolute certainty of divine intervention, especially for miracles of the first of the three categories mentioned above, such as the multiplication of the loaves. However, the difficulty often arises, especially for miracles of the third category, of whether one can ascertain with absolute certainty that the necessary conditions have been met. Can we be absolutely sure, for example, that someone who has apparently come back to life was really dead? It seems that to attain in practice an absolute assurance of the truly miraculous nature of what has occurred, we need to consider carefully not only the first property of miracles, that of surpassing the power of created nature, but also the second, that of being a sign sent by God to man to show him some religious truth.

B. Second reply: the religious context

As well as the physical conditions already discussed, we must necessarily also bear in mind the religious context, before we can have certainty about a miracle. For example, since the apparitions at Lourdes, thousands of sick people have gone there to ask for a healing, and the *Bureau medical des constatations* has declared approximately 2,000 cures to be "scientifically inexplicable" according to the current state of scientific knowledge. However, the ecclesiastical authorities have recognised only seventy of these as miracles, after a thorough canonical investigation.

It is true that some theologians of the late twentieth century went too far in their insistence that miracles must have a religious significance:

> Since a miracle is a sign, some modern authors come to suppose that only this aspect is essential. Provided that some phenomenon is 'significant for my faith', it will be 'miraculous for me'... The fallacy here lies in forgetting that a miracle is a sign precisely because it manifests in an unmistakeable way that God has intervened in the world to guarantee some truth. This is why a miracle must involve some causal act which God alone can perform.[22]

Some modern authors wrongly accuse those theologians who preceded the Second Vatican Council (1962–65) of having neglected the value that miracles possess as *signs*. I am happy, therefore, to be able to quote from a great Dominican and a great Jesuit theologian of the twentieth century, both of them classical Thomists if ever there were, who clearly understood and expressed the idea of miracles as signs that form part of God's governance of creation:

> Signs are a way of participating visibly in what is invisible, and it is natural to man to be instructed in this way. By virtue of his reason, man already participates consciously in a reality that transcends him, and he is unable not to want to know it. He has a natural capacity [...] to discover something transcendent by means of what surrounds him. [...] The argument [based on the principle of causality] cannot convince a person who arbitrarily decides that the human mind can only recognise and synthesise material or formal causes, and who thus reduces the mind to a mere reasoning power. One cannot argue with someone who adopts this position: once a person has warped his own nature, he can no

---

22 Ibid., 257–58.

CHRISTIANITY IS CREDIBLE

longer receive a message consisting in signs which are, precisely, adapted to that nature.[23]

For extraordinary phenomena to be potentially recognised as miraculous, it is necessary first of all that they be *rare*. Thus they will be events which have at least the appearance of originating in some will that has power over its own ends and that can freely choose when to act. Secondly, they must be phenomena capable of being understood in the context of God's governance of the universe so as to *indicate that he is using them as his messengers*. Not only must there be nothing in them which is contrary to right reason or offensive to a well-instructed moral sense, but they also must not be, as it were, 'neutral' or 'silent' events, which have nothing to say to a person who takes religious questions seriously. At the same time, there will need to be some explanation of their meaning. This may take the form of an explicit explanation, which may be given in advance by the one who works the miracle; or, when a miracle has been obtained by the prayers of the faithful, these prayers themselves may be a sufficiently explicit explanation of the significance of what has taken place. Or again, it may be that the holiness of the circumstances in which a miracle occurs renders any further explanation of it unnecessary.[24]

In practice, we may say that the divine authentication of the message given by a miracle-worker is established when:

• the person who works the miracle invokes God, using some prayer which is doctrinally sound, i.e. which contains nothing contrary to reason or to something which has previously been revealed;

• the moral and religious consequences of the miracle are good;

• the miracle takes place in a way that is in harmony with the dignity of God and of man, especially by happening in a manner that is simple and easy to recognise (this criterion

---

23 Michel-Louis Guérard des Lauriers, *Les dimensions de la foi*, Paris, Le Cerf, 1952, vol. 2, pp. 197–98.
24 J. de Tonquédec, *Introduction à l'étude du merveilleux...*, p. 219.

will often enable us to distinguish genuine miracles from diabolic deceits or magic);

• lastly, the miracle-worker is noteworthy for his moral goodness. While it is not impossible that God work a miracle through a sinner, he will in that case make clearly known that the miracle is meant as a testimony not to the man who works it but rather to some truth of which he is a mere messenger.

> True miracles cannot be wrought save by the power of God, because God works them for man's benefit, and this in two ways: in one way for the confirmation of truth declared, in another way in proof of a person's holiness, which God desires to propose as an example of virtue.
>
> In the first way, miracles can be wrought by anyone who preaches the true faith and calls upon Christ's name, as even the wicked do sometimes. In this way, even the wicked can work miracles (cf. Matt. 7:22). [...]
>
> In the second way miracles are not wrought except by the saints, since it is in proof of their holiness that miracles are wrought during their lifetime or after death, either by themselves or by others (cf. Acts 19:11). In this way indeed, there is nothing to prevent a sinner from working miracles by invoking a saint; but the miracle is ascribed not to him, but to the one in proof of whose holiness such things are done.[25]

C. Miracles as proof of doctrine

Miracles constitute a proof of the doctrine in support of which they are worked: not a direct proof, since they do not make us *see* the reality of which the doctrine speaks, but rather an indirect proof. Miracles give us a confidence that some doctrine is true, because the only alternative is the absurd one that an effect exists without a cause. There are, in fact, many miracles where the witnesses possess certainty as to the physical facts, and their testimony can in turn allow others to possess moral or historical certainty. This moral

---

25 St Thomas, STh 2a 2ae 178, 2.

CHRISTIANITY IS CREDIBLE

certainty can also become 'extrinsically' a metaphysical certitude, since it is not possible for a large number of people to agree about a lie for no purpose.

We have already seen this crucial passage from the First Vatican Council, quoted by the *Catechism of the Catholic Church*:

> In order that the obedience of our faith might be in harmony with reason, God willed that to the *interior* help of the Holy Spirit there should be *joined exterior* proofs of his revelation; to wit, divine facts, and *especially miracles* and prophecies, which, as they manifestly display the omnipotence and infinite knowledge of God, are most certain proofs of his divine revelation, adapted to the intelligence of all men.[26]

The anti-modernist oath issued by St Pius X repeats this essential teaching, and adds another important point, namely, that the proof by miracles remains adequate for the modern mind:

> I accept and acknowledge the external proofs of revelation, that is, divine acts and especially miracles and prophecies as most sure signs of the divine origin of the Christian religion and I hold that these same proofs are well *adapted to the understanding of all eras and all men, even those of this time.*[27]

It is nonetheless possible to evade the evidence of miracles, precisely because they are signs and not the realities themselves. Both Cardinal Journet and Fr Guérard des Lauriers emphasise this point rather eloquently:

> A sign may be certain, and even, to an eye-witness, manifest: and yet it may still fail to persuade someone. The evidence of credibility can be resisted. When someone is determined not to lose control over his own life, he will defy any evidence and find reasons why it is unreliable. [...] The evidence of miracles can

---

26 First Vatican Council, Dogmatic Constitution *Dei Filius*, DS 3009; quoted in CCC 156.
27 Apostolic letter *Sacrorum antistitum*, 1st September 1910, DS 3539.

therefore be evaded. Their immediate effect is not to produce faith infallibly, but to attest to the divine origin of some message and thus to provide a rational justification for believing it. Grace, unless it is obstructed, will then cause this message to be accepted. [...] But if a man looks for pretexts not to believe, he will have the misfortune to find them.[28]

A miracle is [...] a kind of salutary surprise, by which I mean a surprise given to us for the sake of our salvation. But it is given only to those people who have not closed themselves off against a reality beyond this world. Or, to express the same thought in a positive way: a person will be able to accept a miracle, and to benefit from it, if he is habitually open to a reality beyond this one. [...] In refusing to work miracles both for the proud man who says that he can do without them, and for the kind of man who tries to live by reasoning alone and who demands them, God is certainly acting freely; yet at the same time, he is also acting in accord with the nature of things, and, in particular, in accord with the nature of a miracle as a *sign*. For the man who encloses himself within his own world is not in a position to perceive a sign of something which wholly transcends him. Signs cannot reach him, as they can reach a man who remains open to a reality beyond.

SECTION II

The miracles of Christ

I. CHRIST PERFORMED 'MIRACLES'

Even a cursory reading of the gospels, and of the other writings of the New Testament which contain the primitive preaching of the apostles (the so-called *kerygma*), shows that *wonders* occupy an important place within them. As I have not yet established their authenticity, I shall refer to them for now as 'miracles', using quotation marks.

The synoptic gospels are full of these wonders, especially the gospel of St Mark, which comes from the preaching of St

---

28 Charles Journet, *Verité de Pascal...*, pp. 222–24.

Peter, who was himself an eye-witness. "In Mark's gospel, the accounts of miracles occupy 31% of the text, or 209 verses out of 666. In the first ten chapters, which describe the public ministry of Jesus before his passion, the proportion is as high as 209 out of 425, or 47%."[29] The first twelve chapters of the gospel of St John are structured around the 'miracles' of Jesus, and the whole gospel concludes with an explicit affirmation of the role played by miracles in Jesus's life: "Jesus did many other signs in the presence of the disciples, which are not written in this book; but these are written that you may believe that Jesus is the Christ, the Son of God, and that believing you may have life in his name" (Jn. 20:30–31).

On the day of Pentecost, during his first sermon to the Jews, Peter appeals to the 'miracles' as a known fact: "Men of Israel, hear these words: Jesus of Nazareth, a man attested to you by God with mighty works and wonders and signs which God did through him in your midst, as you yourselves know [...]" (Acts 2:22). Neither Herod nor the enemies of Jesus denied that he had accomplished wonders, but rather the opposite: "So the chief priests and the Pharisees gathered the council, and said, "What are we to do? For this man performs many signs. If we let him go on thus, everyone will believe in him [...]" (Jn. 11:47–48). Again, the enthusiasm of the people for Jesus could not be accounted for without these 'miracles'.

Hence, anyone who wishes to remain faithful to the historical record must admit the existence of large numbers of wonders in the life of Jesus. This done, such a person can then consider whether these wonders are indeed genuine miracles. But to reject *a priori* the very possibility of miracles in the name of science and objectivity would be to embrace a metaphysical and religious position which is 'reductionist' and as such is lacking objectivity. For science must begin by acknowledging facts. It must acknowledge all the facts, and not set aside some of them in the name of an *a priori* principle of interpretation:

---

29 René Latourelle, *Miracles de Jésus...*, p. 74.

I maintain that *a metaphysical prejudice against the supernatural* crops up constantly in their writings [sc. the writings of those who hold miracles to be impossible *a priori*], even in their textual and literary criticism. This means that whenever they are confronted with statements about miraculous events, they apply a different set of criteria than on other occasions. [...] Provided that we perform our historical criticism properly and systematically, and don't refuse to follow the rules when miracles are in question, then such criticism certainly does not lead us to reject the miracles mentioned by the gospels. It does just the opposite: it places those who deny these miracles in a dilemma, which they can't escape from except by one of those arbitrary leaps of logic which no one would tolerate in any other context.[30]

II. THE PURPOSE OF JESUS'S MIRACLES WAS TO SHOW THE TRUTH OF HIS TEACHING

We should begin by emphasising something of great importance. These 'miracles' were not only wonders surpassing the powers of nature, but also signs bound up with Jesus's mission:

> The signs worked by Jesus attest that the Father has sent him (cf. Jn. 5:36; 10:25). They invite belief in him (cf. Jn. 10:38). To those who turn to him in faith, he grants what they ask (cf. Mk. 5:25–34; 10:52, etc.). So, miracles strengthen faith in the One who does his Father's works; they bear witness that he is the Son of God (cf. Jn. 10:31–38). But his miracles can also be occasions for "offence" (Matt. 11:6); they are not intended to satisfy people's curiosity or desire for magic. Despite his evident miracles some people reject Jesus (cf. Jn. 11:47–48); he is even accused of acting by the power of demons (Mk. 3:22).[31]

It is important to be clear about the connexion between the 'miracles' of Christ and the teaching to the truth of which they bear witness. The fact of this inner bond between teaching and

---

30 E. B. Allo, *Le scandale de Jésus*, Paris, Bernard Grasset, 1927, pp. 59–61.
31 CCC 548.

'miracles' gives to Christianity a unique place in the history of religion. Lacordaire touched on this with his usual eloquence in one of his celebrated 'Conferences of Notre Dame':

> When it comes to historical teachings, by which I mean teachings that were first given by persons of whose existence we can be sure and at a time which is known to history, then I deny purely and simply that any other historical teaching rests on miracles. [...] Someone might allege certain strange events in the history of Greece and Rome. [...] These happenings, whatever we make of them, were but isolated events, without connection to any teaching. They were not 'doctrinal facts', adduced in the proof or discussion of any doctrine. *What we are interested in here, by contrast, are miracles which serve as a foundation for religious doctrines.* For after all, if God manifests himself by certain sovereign acts, this can only be for some great purpose, worthy of himself and of us. It can only be for the sake of the eternal destiny of mankind. [...] Where, then, are the rival teachings, given in full view of history, and established on the basis of miracles? In the history of the world, where is there another power like that of Jesus Christ, or miracles other than those which he worked, or which were worked by the saints who called him Master? We find nothing but a blank: Jesus Christ alone is to be seen, while his enemies, though they may surround him until the end of time, can come up only with doubts, and not with any fact which could be a rival to him, or even comparable to him.[32]

III. JESUS'S MIRACLES MEET THE CRITERIA OF GENUINE HISTORICITY

What are the criteria of genuine historicity in the account of a miracle? They are the same as those by which historians judge in general about whether or not any narration of events is reliable. I shall mention five basic criteria, before speaking also of a sixth, Jesus's 'style' of speaking and acting.

---

[32] Henri-Dominique Lacordaire, 'On the public power of Jesus Christ', *Conferences of Notre Dame*, 38th conference, given in 1846, Paris, Poussielgue, 1906, t. 3, pp. 56–58 (italics added).

1. The first criterion is *multiple attestation*. It is a sign of reliability when testimonies agree with each other, while deriving from different and independent sources. The diversity of sources is well established as regards the testimonies to the miracles of Jesus. This is true even for the synoptic gospels, while it is plain for the other sources — the gospel of St John, the letters of St Paul, and the Acts of the Apostles — both in their relation to the synoptics and in their relation to each other. The contrasts between Jew and Gentile, which influenced the way in which they received the message of Christ, and the fact that the apostles, especially St Paul, had distinct and recognisable personalities, leading them to relate the same events in different ways, enable the independence of the different authors to appear more clearly. Yet all the sources have their basic vocabulary in common, and though they exemplify different kinds of writing, they all clearly agree in affirming that Jesus performed wonders.

2. In what the gospel tells us, we find something which cannot be identified either with the ideas of Judaism or with those of the first Christians: the words and deeds of Jesus. These constitute an episode which is unique in history, thereby fulfilling the second criterion, that of *discontinuity* or *uniqueness*. Jesus's miracles are also part of this uniqueness: whereas the prophets worked their miracles in the name of God, and the apostles will work theirs in the name of Jesus (cf. Acts 3:6 and 9:34), he himself works miracles *in his own name*: "I will; be healed" (Mk. 1:41; cf. Mk. 2:11, 5:41).

3. All exegetes agree that the primary theme in Jesus's preaching is that the 'Kingdom of God' has now arrived. This is mentioned one hundred and four times in the gospels. Words and action of Jesus closely linked to this theme may therefore be considered to be genuine, and these include his parables and miracles. Here we have the criterion of *conformity* which the miracles have with Jesus's essential mission. This conformity can be seen from the fact that he presents the miracles not as mere wonders, but as signs of

the destruction of Satan's kingdom (cf. Lk. 11:17–22) and of the inauguration of God's. Jesus affirms this explicitly, when he performs, in the presence of John the Baptist's messengers, the miracles which had been prophesied as characteristic of the messianic kingdom (Lk. 7:21–22; Is. 26:19, 35:5–6, 42:7, 61:1). He also suggests it implicitly each time that he asks for faith in his Person, come to inaugurate this kingdom, before working a miracle.

4. Another criterion is that of *different presentations* of the same event, owing both to the diverse points of view among the witnesses, and to the different literary forms which they adopt. When some event has really happened, and there is a strong tradition about it, then its very reality will produce a substantial agreement among the witnesses. If they recount it in different ways, this often means that the event is particularly rich in meaning; hence, in writing about it, each author draws attention to different details. But when this divergence of details is joined to unanimity about the central facts, we have a strong argument for historicity. Both in law and in history, absolute identity in the accounts of different witnesses is liable to arouse suspicion, whereas substantial agreement is considered reliable. As examples from the gospel, we have the various accounts of the multiplication of the loaves (for example Mk. 6 and Jn. 6), and of the healing of the epileptic child (Lk. 9; Mk.9; Mt. 17).

5. A criterion which we can call that of *the necessary explanation* is unfortunately often overlooked by exegetes. It is, however, one of the basic principles of any historical reconstruction of the past:

> When we possess a considerable number of facts which stand in need of an adequate and convincing explanation if they are not to remain as enigmas, then if there is only one explanation which sheds light on them and harmonises them (for example, a deed or word or attitude of Jesus), we can conclude that this explanation is the correct one. This criterion allows us to make use of a host of observations, all of which point in the same direction,

Do the miracles of Christ prove his divinity?

and to explain them by means of a 'sufficient reason', that is, some initial fact which accounts for everything else.[33]

In our present question, the 'explanation by miracles' is consistent with what we know. By accepting the proposition, "Jesus of Nazareth worked miracles", we are able to make sense of an impressive variety of historical facts which would otherwise be inexplicable. For example:

- the popular excitement, both during Christ's ministry in Galilee and also before his passion, especially on Palm Sunday;
- the fact that Jesus was considered a prophet (cf. Mk. 8:28);
- the apostles' faith in Jesus as Messiah;
- the large place accorded to accounts of miracles in the gospels, both in the synoptics and in St John;
- the attitude of the high-priests and of the Pharisees in regard to the wonders;
- the linking of miracles to the coming of the kingdom;
- the primitive *kerygma*, in which the apostles present Jesus as Messiah precisely in virtue of his miracles (Acts 2:22);
- the fact that such miracles would fit well with a host of other equally great signs which Jesus gave, in particular, the fulfilment of the prophecies of the Old Testament, the unique depth of his teaching, and the supreme sign, his own resurrection;[34]
- finally, Jesus's intention to show that he knows the Father, and that he can forgive sins and save people, in proof of all of which he put forward the signs which he is accomplishing (cf. Lk 5:24; Jn. 15:24).

It is impossible to understand any of these things if one rejects the reality of his miracles, while if one accepts the miracles, all these things make sense.

---

33 R. Latourelle, *L'accès à Jésus par les Évangiles*, pp. 88–89.
34 I spoke of the fulfilment of the prophecies in the previous chapter; I shall speak below of the other two signs, which are also of great importance, that is, the teaching of Jesus and his resurrection.

We may note that the five criteria of historicity reinforce each other. The fact that they are all present in the gospel accounts of the miracles is highly impressive, and it is difficult to reject the solid evidence for historicity which this creates. Of course, I do not expect this argument to convince someone who refuses on principle the idea of God's intervening in human history, although it may prompt him to reflect whether his prejudice is well-founded. And if a person does not close his mind and heart to the very possibility of the supernatural, he can see how the argument from history attests to the reality of a divine intervention, and he can thus be spiritually disposed to receive the grace of faith. For a person who already believes, the historical argument demonstrates the harmony of faith and reason and helps him to see more deeply the *unity* of God's saving message. By his miracles, Christ was allowing something of the mystery of his Person to be glimpsed in human history: the mystery that He is Wisdom, Power, and Love.

IV. The 'style' of Jesus's miracles

The manner in which Jesus works his miracles is worth noting. He is always calm, and he works only miracles which are worthy to be performed. This is in striking contrast with the apocryphal gospels, which abound in wonders worked for their own sake. For example, in the 'gospel of Thomas', Jesus is portrayed as a whimsical child who loves to show his superiority over other children of his own age, making birds from clay and then giving life to them, punishing his teachers, and even correcting imperfections in St Joseph's handiwork!

Jesus's miracles are not intended to bring glory to him as their author, unlike in the Hellenistic world, where wonderful works always serve to glorify some hero, by emphasising either how powerful he is, or how he enjoys the protection of the gods. The miracles of Jesus, by contrast, are always worked for the good of others.[35] He never refuses to cure those who

---

35 Pierre Benoit provides an enlightening comparison between the miracles of Jesus and the wonders attributed to certain gods or sages

are suffering, when he is asked; but during the temptation in the desert, he will not work miracles to sate his own hunger, or to gain a spectacular glory for himself in the presence of the Jews gathered in the temple, or to acquire dominion over the world (Lk. 4:1–13). Likewise, in the Garden of Olives, although he declares that he would have the power to do so, he does not request his Father to send him twelve legions of angels to protect him from his enemies (cf. Matt. 26:53). Neither, with the single exception of the withering of the fig tree, an event which had a symbolic meaning (cf. Mk 11:12–14, 20–21), does Christ work punitive wonders in order to alarm people or to govern them by fear; and he does not allow his apostles to call down fire from heaven upon the Samaritans who would not receive him (cf. Lk. 9:51–56).

Jesus acts very simply, and with perfect self-command. There are no trances or ecstasies. He does not employ lengthy prayers, magical formulas, hypnosis or suggestion. At most he may use a symbolic gesture: but a single word or command is sufficient to produce the miraculous effect. The cures are generally instantaneous, even when worked at a distance, although we can note that a few of them occur by stages, in order to teach something more effectively, as for example the healing of the blind man of Bethsaida (cf. Mk. 8:22–25):

> This was certainly a miracle, and yet it was not dramatic. It does not seem that Mark recounted it in order to explain the confession of Peter [which follows immediately]. Yet it was an act of Jesus, and so, like all his actions, it must have some meaning. A gradual increase of light is the natural symbol of a progress in understanding. Since the blind man recovered his sight only by degrees, we need not be surprised that Christ's instructions took hold only gradually of the minds of the disciples. But they would see clearly in the end, and then they would also understand how it was from wisdom that he had taught them so slowly.[36]

---

in Greek antiquity, such as Apollonius of Tyana; *Exégèse et théologie*, vol. 1, Paris, Le Cerf, 1961, pp. 120–24.

36 Marie-Joseph Lagrange, *L'Évangile de Jésus-Christ...*, p. 280.

Jesus's wonders, moreover, are always performed in a religious context. I have already emphasised that miracles are signs manifesting an encounter with the kingdom of God, which, in Jesus, irrupts into the world, as well as instruments to effect this encounter. I shall return this point, as it is a key one.

Finally, his miracles have about them something rather 'discreet' — for example, he often asks those who have benefitted from them to say nothing. He works them only for the genuine good of those who ask from faith. He will not satisfy the curiosity of Herod, who wanted to enjoy some astonishing sight (cf. Lk. 23:8–11), nor will he give the Pharisees their great sign in the heavens (cf. Matt. 16:1–4). He knows when the people asking for miracles are badly disposed and would become still more blind and blameworthy if they were to see a marvellous display of power.

V. JESUS'S MIRACLES PROVE THAT HE IS GOD'S MESSENGER

> Jesus did not simply speak; he proved his words by actions. This was necessary in order that he might justify both his extraordinary claims and the unconditional attachment to his own Person which he required. [...] When Jesus works miracles, he works them as 'signs' which will lead people to see them as something more than simple wonders. What he requires, or what moves him to work a miracle, is faith in his own Person, and in the mission which God will thereby confirm. The question, therefore, is 'what is he claiming to be, when he performs such signs to support his own words?' For if the miracles are genuine, they prove whatever they are intended to prove.[37]

Jesus claimed, very clearly, to be inaugurating the messianic age and the kingdom of God. He also affirmed his sovereign authority over the Law itself and required an entire faith in his own person and mission. This is why the crowds hailed him as the Son of David. Again, Peter's confession at

---

37 P. Benoit, *Exégèse et théologie*, pp. 120, 124.

Caesarea Philippi indicates at the very least his own faith that Jesus is the Messiah. Hence, Jesus's miracles establish that he showed himself to be the Messiah, the messenger of God.

VI. JESUS'S MIRACLES PROVE THAT HE IS THE SON OF GOD

Yet, "we find in the Gospel clear signs that Jesus went beyond ordinary messianism in the claims that he made",[38] thus preparing the disciples to come to faith in their master's divinity, a faith that would be firmly established by his resurrection. There is in the gospels a kind of gradation to Jesus's affirmation of his own identity. This process reaches its climax in the affirmation of his divinity made in an official manner before the Sanhedrin. The trial was getting nowhere, and so the high priest rose and, with these piercing words, adjured Jesus to unveil his identity: "I adjure thee by the living God to tell us if thou are the Christ, the Son of God" (Matt. 26:63).[39] It is a formal act, issuing from the highest religious authority; everything will depend on what happens now. How can Jesus keep silent, as he has kept silent during the false and self-contradictory accusations which have been made against him thus far?

The Saviour's reply, however, is much more than a simple declaration of his messiahship. The question that was posed related directly to the title of 'Messiah'. He accepts this title unequivocally, yet without dwelling on it, with the words, "Thou hast said so" (Matt. 26:64).[40] But there could be no *blasphemy* in simply declaring oneself to be the Messiah whom God had promised to send his people. Yet Jesus gives a meaning to the title 'Son of God' which goes beyond the adoptive filiation that would belong to a merely human Messiah:

> "You have said so. But I tell you, hereafter you will see the Son of man seated at the right hand of Power, and

---

38 Ibid., p. 126.
39 Cf. Mk. 14:61, "The Christ, the Son of the Blessed one".
40 Cf. Lk. 22:70: "I am".

coming on the clouds of heaven" (Matt. 26:64). But why at these words did the high priest cry out: "He has blasphemed"? Why did the members of the Sanhedrin immediately declare: "He deserves to die" (Matt. 26:65, 68)? It is because, in the presence of the highest authorities of his people, Jesus has affirmed himself here to be *equal to God*. Those who hated him were able to see his meaning, veiled though it was. Love should not be less perceptive than hatred.[41]

The Law recognised three forms of blasphemy. Jesus was clearly not guilty of the first two, since he neither cursed God nor used the Name of God (YHWH), employing instead a common Jewish expression, "the Power". To be open, therefore, to a charge of blasphemy, he must have ascribed a divine attribute to himself. Being "seated at the right hand" of God signified being equal to him. Jesus identifies himself as the Son of Man prophesied by Daniel: "Thrones were placed, and one that was ancient of days took his seat [...] Behold, with the clouds of heaven there came one like a son of man, and he came to the Ancient of Days and was presented before him" (Dan. 7:9, 13). He joins this prophecy with that of psalm 110 [109]: "The Lord said to my Lord, Sit on my right."

By bringing together these two mysterious passages of Scripture, Jesus makes each of them shed light on the other. The "sitting at the right hand" which the psalmist mentions as a privilege of the Messiah had been interpreted by the rabbis in a figurative way. They said the Messiah would live in the South Palace, on the right side of the temple. By speaking of his coming with the clouds, Jesus gives a quite different sense to the phrase: the sitting is no longer a metaphor, pertaining to this world, but a real sitting in heaven. Again, according to Jesus's declaration, the Son of Man will not only be brought toward the throne of the Ancient of Days, that is, toward God in his eternity, but he will sit at his right, occupying one of the thrones to which Daniel referred. "Henceforth,

---

41 Paul Lamarche, *Christ vivant, Essai sur la christologie du Nouveau Testament*, Le Cerf, *Lectio divina* collection, n. 43, Paris, 1966, p. 153.

the Son of Man will be enthroned at the right hand of the power of God" (Lk. 22:69).

> If Jesus's reply appeared blasphemous, this was not on account of either of the texts in themselves, but on account of the declaration that resulted from the union of the two texts. [...] To sit metaphorically could belong to a man; to sit in heaven in reality would mean that Jesus was equal to God, and this was the 'blasphemy'.[42]

This is why, when the Jews bring Jesus to Pilate, they say: "We have a Law, and by this Law he ought to die, since he has made himself the Son of God" (Jn. 19:7).

> The decisive point was the way in which Jesus phrased his answer. He solemnly identifies himself with the mysterious Son of man whom the prophet Daniel beheld in a vision and to whom God bestowed an eternal empire (Dan. 7:13–14), and he emphasises the transcendent character of this title by further declaring that he, Jesus, the Son of man whom Daniel foretold, would sit at the right hand of the Almighty and come on the clouds of heaven. In the Old Testament, the Power and the clouds are strictly divine attributes. By applying them to himself, Jesus is clearly claiming divine rank, and he can thus be accused of encroaching on the prerogatives of God himself. The high priest of the Sanhedrin does not mistake his meaning, and he immediately condemns Jesus for blasphemy [...].[43]

Accordingly, the New Testament, and the creed in the Catholic liturgy, make this "sitting at the right hand of God" the expression of Jesus's divinity: "The Lord Jesus, when he had spoken to them, was taken up into heaven and sat at the right hand of God" (Mk. 16:19).

But as the angelic doctor states:

> It cannot happen that a man who preaches a false doctrine works true miracles, for such miracles cannot be

---

[42] P. Lamarche, *Christ vivant*..., p. 155.
[43] André Léonard, *Les raisons de croire*, Communio/Sarment, Éditions du Jubilé, 2010, p. 100.

done without divine power, and so God would then bear witness to a falsehood, which is impossible. Therefore, since Christ said that he was the Son of God, and equal to God, the miracles which he did prove the truth of this teaching.[44]

Therefore, when we consider that Christ clearly, though implicitly, affirmed his divinity, and when we consider his miracles in this light, our mind may attain with certainty to the fact that he is God.[45]

---

[44] St Thomas Aquinas, *Quodlibetal questions*, II.4, a. 1 ad 4: "Sed hoc contingere non potest quod aliquis falsam doctrinam annuntians, vera miracula faciat, quae nisi virtute divina fieri non possunt; sic enim Deus esset falsitatis testis, quod est impossibile. Cum ergo Christus se filium Dei diceret, et aequalem Deo, hanc eius doctrinam comprobabant miracula quae faciebat; et ideo ostendebatur Christus per miracula quae faciebat, esse Deus."
[45] It is an indirect proof by means of a sure sign; cf. p. 46 above. [this will need to be changed.]

CHAPTER 4

Does the excellence of Christian doctrine show its divine origin?

SECTION I

Christ's doctrinal mission

I. JESUS TRULY TAUGHT

We live in a context both of scepticism about the capacities of the intellect and of distrust of dogma, the latter often being seen as the cause of religious fanaticism. For this reason, the first task of this chapter will be to establish that Jesus of Nazareth truly *taught*.

Both the concealed anti-intellectualism of the modern world and the Modernist idea of religious sentiment tend to create an opposition between what is doctrinal and what is personal. We often hear people say: "Christians follow a person (Christ) more than a doctrine"; or even, "a person *rather than* a doctrine". The latter expression is heretical; anyone who does not adhere to the creed, which is a series of propositions revealed by God, does not have the Catholic faith. The former expression is imprecise and could serve to undermine the indispensable place of doctrine in Christianity. It is in fact doctrine which brings us to Christ and allows us to adhere to the mystery of his person, through the theological virtues and the gifts of the Holy Ghost. It certainly exceeds the capacity of any finite intellect fully to grasp and describe Christ's person, since his person is divine; yet it is not possible to adhere to the mystery of Christ except by means of revelation, and revelation is given to the *intellect*, itself elevated by means of faith and perfected by the gifts of understanding and wisdom. If "Christ does not dwell in our hearts by faith", then we are not able "to know the love of Christ which surpasses all knowledge" (cf. Eph. 3:17–19). The words with which St Catherine of Siena began her celebrated *Dialogue* are not only true, but also very pertinent to our times: "Love follows knowledge, and when a soul loves, she seeks to follow the truth and to be clad in truth."[1]

A. Jesus fulfilled the Messiah's doctrinal mission

In a previous chapter, we saw how Jesus of Nazareth, by fulfilling the prophecies of the Old Testament, showed that he was indeed the Messiah. But it is certain that the Messiah was supposed to be a prophet, who would accomplish the task of teaching in the name of God:

> The Lord your God will raise up for you a prophet like me from among you, from your brethren—him you shall heed—just as you desired of the Lord your God at Horeb on the day of the assembly, when you said, 'Let me not hear again the voice of the Lord my God, or see this great fire any more, lest I die.' And the Lord said to me, 'They have rightly said all that they have spoken. I will raise up for them a prophet like you from among their brethren; and I will put my words in his mouth, and he shall speak to them all that I command him. And whoever will not give heed to my words which he shall speak in my name, I myself will require it of him (Deut. 18:15–19).

At the time of Jesus it was well understood, even by Samaritans, that the Messiah would have a doctrinal role. The Samaritan woman who spoke to Jesus at the well of Jacob says to him plainly: "I know that the Messiah is coming, who is called Christ. When he comes, he will explain all things." And Jesus replied: "I who speak to you am he" (Jn. 4:25–26).

Again, the sacred texts, especially the psalms and Isaiah, present the Messiah as not only a Master, or as a rabbi in Israel, but as the Teacher of all the nations:

> The Lord hath said to me: Thou art my son, this day have I begotten thee. Ask of me, and I will give thee the Gentiles for thy inheritance, and the utmost parts

---

[1] St Catherine of Siena, *Dialogue*, ch. 1.

of the earth for thy possession. Thou shalt rule them with a rod of iron, and shalt break them in pieces like a potter's vessel. And now, O ye kings, understand: *receive instruction*, you that judge the earth (Ps. 2:7–10).

In the last days the mountain of the house of the Lord shall be prepared on the top of mountains, and it shall be exalted above the hills, and all nations shall flow unto it. And many people shall go, and say: Come and let us go up to the mountain of the Lord, and to the house of the God of Jacob, and *he will teach us his ways*, and we will walk in his paths: for the law shall come forth from Sion, and the word of the Lord from Jerusalem (Is. 2:2–3).

Other passages from the same prophet are equally relevant: "[...] Your teacher will not hide himself any more, but your eyes shall see your teacher" (Is. 30:20). "The bruised reed he shall not break, and smoking flax he shall not quench: he shall bring forth judgment unto truth. He shall not be sad, nor troublesome, till he set judgment in the earth: and the islands shall wait for his law" (Is. 42:3–4). "It is too light a thing that you should be my servant to raise up the tribes of Jacob and to restore the preserved of Israel; I will give you as a light to the nations, that my salvation may reach to the end of the earth" (Is. 49:6).

B. Jesus accepted the title of Teacher

Jesus accepted the title of 'Teacher' unambiguously. He makes no protest when Nicodemus addresses him thus; on the contrary, he immediately initiates a deep doctrinal discussion. "There was a man of the Pharisees, named Nicodemus, a ruler of the Jews. This man came to Jesus by night, and said to him: Rabbi, we know that thou art come a teacher from God; for no man can do these signs which thou dost, unless God be with him" (Jn. 3:1–2). Jesus allows himself on several occasions to be called "Teacher" by the Pharisees,[2] and he replies clearly to moral and doctrinal questions. Here

---

2   Cf. Matt 8:19, 9:11, 12:38, 17:24, 19:16, 22:24, 22:36.

are two examples: "And they sent their disciples to him, along with the Herodians, saying, "Teacher, we know that you are true, and teach the way of God truthfully, and care for no man; for you do not regard the position of men. Tell us, then, what you think. Is it lawful to pay taxes to Caesar, or not?" (Matt. 22:16–17). "When the Pharisees heard that he had silenced the Sadducees, they came together. And one of them, a lawyer, asked him a question, to test him. "Teacher, which is the great commandment in the law?"" (Matt. 22:34–36).

Jesus of Nazareth also explicitly referred to himself as a Teacher: "You call me Teacher and Lord; and you are right, for so I am" (Jn. 13:13). He even taught that he was the only Teacher, in the full and proper sense of the term[3]: "Be not you called Rabbi. For one is your master; and all you are brethren. And call none your father upon earth; for one is your father, who is in heaven. Neither be ye called masters; for one is your master, Christ" (Matt. 23:8–10).

C. Jesus dedicates himself to teaching

Jesus affirmed that he had been sent by the Father to preach a doctrine which comes from the Father. "My doctrine is not mine, but his that sent me" (Jn. 7:16). "For I have not

---

[3] God is the only Teacher in the proper sense of the term, since only he draws his teaching from within himself, and enlightens the mind of his disciples interiorly. Human teachers are teachers only in a ministerial sense: their teaching comes from the first truth, and they assist the disciple to make his own act of understanding, just as a doctor merely assists nature, and helps it to perform its proper activity, so that healing may occur. St Thomas comments on this passage of St Matthew's gospel as follows: "We should say that the one who is called teacher in the proper sense is the one who has his doctrine from himself, not the one who dispenses to others a doctrine which has been passed on to him. And thus, there is only one teacher, namely God, who properly speaking possesses his doctrine, although there are many who are teachers in an instrumental way. [...] Chrysostom says that just as there is one God by nature, but many are gods by participation, so also there is only one teacher naturally, but many instrumentally. [...] Knowledge is like health, for it has a principle within ourselves, namely, the intellect; the one who teaches offers some help towards acquiring a doctrine, as the doctor offers some help towards acquiring health; but only God acts inwardly in the intellect" (*In Matthaeum,* cap. 23, Marietti, no. 1848–49).

spoken of myself; but the Father who sent me, he gave me commandment what I should say, and what I should speak" (Jn. 12:49). We see in the gospel that he dedicates his time principally to the mission of teaching, by preaching the kingdom of God, which means announcing good news, that is, 'evangelising'. "When it was day, he departed and went into a lonely place. And the people sought him and came to him, and would have kept him from leaving them; but he said to them, 'I must preach the good news of the kingdom of God to the other cities also; for I was sent for this purpose'. And he was preaching in the synagogues of Judea" (Lk. 4:42–44).

Jesus presents himself as *light*: "I am the way, the truth and the life" (Jn. 14:6). He attributes so great an importance to his teaching mission, that he makes it a condition of salvation for all men that they accept his doctrine (Jn. 3:18). He then passes on this mission to his disciples: "And he said to them, 'Go into all the world and preach the gospel to the whole creation. He who believes and is baptized will be saved; but he who does not believe will be condemned'" (Mk. 16:5–16). The apostle of the gentiles tells us that this doctrine must be treated as a sacred deposit (cf. 1 Tim. 6:20).

Jesus of Nazareth recalled to people's knowledge certain natural truths about religion which had become obscured with time, and he also taught profound mysteries.[4] It is therefore false to claim, with the Modernists, that "Christ did not teach a determined body of doctrine applicable to all times and all men, but rather inaugurated a religious movement adapted or to be adapted to different times and places".[5] This is an error which corresponded to the visceral anti-intellectualism of the Modernist movement, and to their erroneous conception of truth: they defined truth not as the conformity of the intellect to reality (*adæquatio rei et intellectus*), but as an "adequation of intellect with life".

---

[4] I shall speak of the content of his teaching in the second part of this chapter.
[5] Pope St Pius X condemned this error in 1907, in the decree *Lamentabili*, DS 3459.

II. CHRIST PREACHED IN AN ADMIRABLE MANNER

The gospel's extraordinary influence derives in part from the manner in which Jesus preached. His words enlighten his hearers by their simplicity. His words are infused, too, with a spiritual quality that moves men's hearts. But they also carry conviction, being spoken with authority.[6]

A. *A simplicity that enlightens his hearers*

Jesus knew how to evangelise the poor, and without the abstract language of philosophers. His words are indeed "spirit and life" (Jn. 6:63). Guiding souls has been called "the art of arts": *ars artium, regimen animarum*. It involves explaining the greatest mysteries about God and creation to people of all conditions, without driving anyone beyond his capacities. It means helping people to begin to see that the road that leads to salvation is difficult, yet without dismaying them. Jesus did all this with supreme ease. His pedagogy was perfect. If we look at the intellectual history of mankind, we generally find that teachers pass on their wisdom to a few chosen disciples, thus creating a kind of intellectual aristocracy whose doctrines often have a slightly esoteric air. Compared to this, Jesus's preaching is a kind of moral miracle. People from humble backgrounds become wise: they discover the 'true philosophy' and enter the way of salvation, just as much as the greatest of his followers.

For twenty centuries, Jesus's teaching has been the principle and inspiration of millions of people's lives in every generation.

> There is a man over whose tomb love keeps watch. [...] There is a man whose steps a considerable portion of mankind follows, without growing weary [...] There is a man who died and was buried, but in whose very sleep and waking men are keenly interested, and whose every word still resonates among us, effecting something

---

6 Cf. St Thomas, STh 2a 2ae 171, 1: the preacher must instruct men, move them and convince them.

greater even than love - namely, virtues which blossom into love's perfection. [...] There is a man, pursued by never-ending hatred even unto torture and the tomb, who looks for apostles and martyrs in each new generation as it arises; and in every generation, he finds them.[7]

This teaching given to the poor is also one of the messianic signs which Jesus mentions at the very start of his preaching, with a quotation from the prophet Isaiah (Is. 61:1), both in the synagogue at Nazareth, and again to the messengers of John the Baptist: "The poor are evangelised" (Matt. 11:5; Lk. 7:22). Jesus's teaching is in keeping with his humility as a teacher who does not seek marks of honour and "the first seats" (cf. Matt. 23:1–12), and who turns people's attention from himself to the message which he brings (cf. Jn. 7:16).

Unlike many prophets, Jesus does not grow *excited*; however sublime may be the theme of his preaching, he is always calm:

> Who can fail to admire the way in which he brings the highest truths down to our level? His teaching is milk for the little ones, and at the same time bread for the strong. We can see that he knows the secrets of God, and yet that he does not marvel at them, as other mortals do to whom God has spoken. He speaks about them very naturally; he is born to them, as it were, and born to glory. That which "he has without measure" (Jn. 3:34), he bestows in a measured way, and so our weakness is able to receive it.[8]

B. A power to touch the heart

Jesus's preaching has nothing in common with the sentimentality of the Romantic movement, and yet, even when he is speaking of difficult or austere things, he does not speak austerely, but from the heart. His preaching perfectly exemplifies what he himself says concerning man's speech: "From

---

7 Lacordaire, *Conferences of Notre Dame*, 39th conference, given in 1846, Paris, Poussielgue, 1906, vol. 3, pp. 73–74.
8 Bossuet, *Discours sur l'histoire universelle*, part 2, ch. 19, in *Œuvres complètes*, Vivès, vol. XXIV, p. 449.

the abundance of the heart, the mouth speaks" (Matt. 12:34). We feel that his inner life, as a man, corresponds perfectly to his words, and that his life is imbued with the same divine love of which he speaks to others. There is nothing artificial or unnatural about the manner in which he reacts to the people and things around him. He encourages souls toward salvation by a charity and a goodness which flow from himself spontaneously. We see this, for example, in his conversation with the Samaritan woman: "If you knew the gift of God..." (Jn. 4:1); and also with the woman caught in adultery: "Neither do I condemn you. Go, and sin no more" (Jn. 8:11).

Jesus is not unwilling to show his capacity for feeling and for love. He works his first miracle at a wedding banquet, to save his hosts from shame (Jn. 2:1–11). He takes thought for the bodily needs of his disciples when they are over-worked (Mk. 6:31) or worn out by fishing (Jn. 21:9). He has a particular love for John (Jn. 13:23, 21:20), and for the family of Bethany (Jn. 11:5). He is touched by the sight of the crowd who are like sheep without a shepherd (Mk. 6:34), and he feels compassion upon seeing the widow who has lost her only son (Lk. 7:13). He groans and weeps when he draws near to the tomb of his friend Lazarus (Jn. 11:35). He is filled with joy in thinking of the divine revelation which he is bringing to the humble (Lk. 10:21). He speaks openly of the distress which he suffers at the thought of his future 'baptism of blood', the passion (Lk. 12:50). He is troubled within himself at the thought of Judas's treachery (Jn. 13:21).

Christ's "measureless love for mankind"[9] appears in his words, and touches people's hearts. The woman in the crowd who is mentioned by St Luke clearly felt this appeal, when she

---

9 In the liturgy of St John Chrysostom, during the beautiful prayer known as the *Cherubikon*, the priest addresses Christ in these terms: "On account of Thy ineffable and measureless love for man (*dià tēn áphaton kaì amétrētón sou philanthrōpían*), Thou didst become man without change or alteration; Thou didst become our high priest, and Thou hast bestowed upon us the sacrifice of this spiritual and unbloody oblation, being the Master of all things."

was moved to call out to Christ, in a very womanly, and very Semitic, way: "As he said this, a woman in the crowd raised her voice and said to him, 'Blessed is the womb that bore you, and the breasts that you sucked!'" (Lk. 11:27). Yet men also feel his power of attraction, for example, the attendants who were sent to arrest him in the Temple during the feast of Tabernacles: "No man ever spoke like this man" (Jn. 7:46).

If "the crowds were full of admiration at his teaching" (Mt. 22:33), what must have been the effect produced on the disciples by his discourse after the last Supper? "These last words of his are like so many sheets or waves of light, which come down from heaven and will continue to spread across all future generations, like ever-expanding circles".[10] Romano Guardini spoke in a restrained yet moving manner about this last discourse, which he said expressed the overflow of the 'circular contemplation' of Christ's heart:[11]

> Then, in the fourteenth and fifteenth chapters of St. John, come the sacred passages about love, reiterated and deepened again and again. The love in question is no mere philanthropy or general love of goodness and truth, but a love which is possible only through him, Jesus Christ; a love that is directed to the Father and returns from him to our fellow-men.[12]

Speaking of the 'priestly prayer' of chapter seventeen of St John, Guardini writes:

> It is one of the holiest passages of the New Testament [...] There is no logical sequence of thought, no because and therefore, but a simpler—or more complicated—pattern. A thought emerges and sinks back into the depths. A second appears, disappears, and the first returns. [...] What is revealed is not any chain of thought, but a fundamental reality, a truth, a plenitude

---

[10] R. Garrigou-Lagrange, *Le Sauveur et son amour pour nous*, Juvisy, Cerf, 1933, p. 183.
[11] On the three 'movements of contemplation', cf. Dionysius, *The Divine Names*, ch. 4 §§ 8 and 9.
[12] R. Guardini, *Le Seigneur*, Paris, Alsatia, 1945, vol. 2, pp. 62–63; English version: *The Lord*, Gateway Editions, 1996, p. 416.

of heart that ebbs and flows like the tides of a deep sea. The point of departure-and-return is the union of Jesus' human heart and spirit with his living divinity. Jesus' words must be read and retained; the new sentences constantly fused with those before. One most grope behind every thought deep into the inexpressible from which it rises, noting how the ineffable breaks through again and again in ever different form.[13]

C. An authority that carries conviction

The preaching of Jesus does not only enlighten people's minds and engage their emotions, but also moves their will by its great authoritativeness. St Matthew notes: "The crowds were full of admiration at his teaching, for he taught them as one having authority, and not like their scribes" (Matt. 7:28–29). The scribes made their teaching rest on the authority of earlier teachers, whereas Jesus's is like that of God himself, speaking to Moses or to one of the prophets. This is evident in the five places in the Sermon on the Mount when he brings to perfection some part of the first covenant. "You have heard that *it was said*... but I say to you" (Matt. 5:21–42). The 'divine passive', *it was said,* is a reference to the promulgation of the ten commandments by God on Mount Sinai.

But who else has ever asked people to listen to him as they would to God? "You believe in God, believe also in me" (Jn. 14:1). Who has ventured to claim, like Jesus, to be the only person to know who God is? "No one knows the Father except the Son" (Matt. 11:27; cf. Lk. 10:22). Christ's teaching, unlike that of the rabbis, does not consist essentially in the interpretation of Scripture. Rather, it is a communication of new truths, which are often introduced by the powerful phrase, "Amen, amen, I say to you".[14] Jesus affirms that he speaks of something of which he has a personal knowledge: "I tell you that which I have seen with my Father" (Jn. 8:38). Who else has ever dared to assert that he will attract to

---

13 R. Guardini, *Le Seigneur,* pp. 83–84; *The Lord,* pp. 437–438.
14 The double 'Amen' is characteristic of St John's gospel. In the synoptics, we find: "Amen, I say to you".

himself every heart that is open to the truth? "Whoever is of the truth hears my voice" (Jn. 18:37).

As he begins his work of preaching, Jesus "is aware of being beyond the judgements of men: beyond their enquiries or criticisms or contradictions".[15] He gives them to understand that his authority surpasses that of Jonah or Solomon (cf. Matt. 12:38–42). While he can enter into discussions and into sometimes strongly-worded disputations, he nevertheless directs them where he wills. He always remains the master during these conversations, and those who contradict him "are filled with wonder at his reply and remain silent" (Lk. 20:26), to such a point that "no one dares ask him any more questions" (Mk. 12:34).

He does not normally use rhetorical devices or abstract arguments when he preaches. Instead, he speaks straightforwardly, using simple phrases and vivid images. Although what he says may be difficult to accept for those who are under the sway of their unruly emotions, his words resonate with the deepest desires of the human heart. Even people who are wilful by nature, or hard to please, find the words and images of Jesus to be penetrating and powerful, like a ray of light or a surgical cauterisation. If his words are so memorable, this is not only because they employ certain techniques, at which the Jewish rabbis excelled, to render memorisation easy, but also because of the pure gracefulness of the imagery which he employs:

> Jesus has the urgency, and the forcefulness, of the prophets, yet he also has the composure and the clarity of the sage. In speaking of God and of the kingdom of God, he uses parables which have been acknowledged ever since as monuments of good sense, which put the highest thoughts within reach of an audience composed of fishermen, farmers, and shepherds. Jewish scholars find it hard to discover anything in the Talmud which could be compared with them. Of course, Jesus spoke the language of his time, but he spoke it as no one

---

15 R. Garrigou-Lagrange, *Le Sauveur et son amour pour nous*, p. 180.

else did: so beautifully and so movingly, and yet with a naturalness which one might almost call casual did it not pierce one to the very heart.[16]

We feel that his words are that "sharp, double-edged sword" which John, in the visions of the Apocalypse, sees coming from the mouth of the Son of man, and which "pierces even to the division of soul and spirit" (Heb. 4:12). We cannot remain neutral when we hear his words. They reveal the contents of men's hearts. Even those who are determined to reject them are obliged to acknowledge their power: "If we leave him thus, everyone will believe in him" (Jn. 11:47). Why is this? Jesus's own holiness, as well as his undeniable miracles, is an irresistible confirmation of his preaching. He was speaking, on one occasion, to a group of intelligent enemies who were full of jealousy toward him and who had been watching him for months with that terrible perceptiveness which hatred sometimes gives a person about what he hates. In such circumstances, would any other teacher have said: "Which of you will convict me of sin?" (Jn. 8:46). But Jesus can do so, since "he did and taught" (Acts 1:1). The incarnate Word is himself a 'living standard' against which his own words may be measured.

SECTION II

The sublimity of Christ's doctrine

1. THE 'DIMENSIONS' OF CHRISTIAN DOCTRINE

The Apostle of the gentiles has a lyrical passage, full of energy, in which he describes the vastness of the mystery of Christ. It is a mystery into which those who believe in Christ may freely enter, because a lover always has a kind of affinity with that which he loves:

> For this reason I bow my knees before the Father, from whom every family in heaven and on earth is named, that according to the riches of his glory he may grant you to be strengthened with might through his Spirit in

---

16 Marie-Joseph Lagrange, *L'Évangile de Jésus-Christ...*, p. 655.

the inner man, and that Christ may dwell in your hearts through faith; that you, being rooted and grounded in love, may have power to comprehend with all the saints what is the breadth and length and height and depth, and to know the love of Christ which surpasses knowledge, that you may be filled with all the fulness of God (Eph. 3:14–19).

Since this is a work of apologetics, I shall try to set forth the content of Christian teaching as it is knowable to a person of good faith who studies the writings of the New Testament in an unprejudiced way. My ideal reader is also someone who does not reject on principle the clarifications about Christian belief that have been provided by the Catholic magisterium: for the Church's magisterium can certainly be considered, simply in human terms, as possessing a specialised knowledge of the body of Christian writings. If we look in this way at "the breadth, the length, the height and the depth" (Eph. 3:18) of Christ's doctrine, contemplating it as it were from outside, what do we see?

A. Natural truths about God and man

NATURAL THEOLOGY. Christ's doctrine concerning God agrees with what natural reason is able to establish with certitude. When religions and philosophers speak of 'God', they mean a Being who is unique, the beginning and end of all other beings, who exists by himself, is eternal and everywhere present, infinitely perfect, really distinct from the world, who governs the world, and is wise and all-powerful. These attributes seem to be already found implicitly, when natural reason conceives God as 'the one who made the world and who possesses all perfections'. They are likewise accepted, more or less, by all those philosophers who are not radically atheistic, which means the majority of them: for the modern atheistic materialism of the western world is something exceptional, if one considers the length and breadth of human history. In fact, many agnostic or atheistic thinkers indirectly bear witness to the idea of God just described, in that they implicitly admit that if he exists, he must have these attributes which the 'perennial philosophy' ascribes to him. If these thinkers reject God, this is often because they cannot see how the existence of such a Being is compatible with the fact of evil in the world, or perhaps with human freedom.

Yet Christianity affirms these divine attributes with a clarity and a precision that is unequalled outside Christianity. The Old and the New Testament tell us that God is in himself unique (Mk. 12:29, where Jesus quotes from Deut. 6:4), a pure spirit (Jn. 4:21), who exists of himself (Ex. 3:14), who is eternal (Rom. 16:26; Apoc. 1:8), present everywhere and in all things (Mt. 5:34; Acts 7:49), wise (Rom. 11:33, 16:27), and all-powerful (Matt. 19:26; Eph. 3:20; Acts 4:24, 14:15). God, in his freedom (Eph. 1:1; Rom. 9:16), created all beings (Acts 4:24, 14:14; Eph. 3:9; Apoc. 1:8) and keeps them in existence (Heb. 1:3). This doctrine of the entire liberty of God's act of creation means that Christianity is unlike Buddhism, or the other religions of the Far East, or emanationist philosophies,[17] since it is free from any trace of pantheism. It is also entirely unlike any of the various forms of dualism, whether we think of the Platonic theory of uncreated matter, or of the ancient Persian religion, with its two supreme principles, one good and one evil. Christian doctrine is likewise opposed to the determinism that would see creation as a moral necessity, required if God is to be truly perfect.

God is the good and provident ruler of the world which he has made (Matt. 6:26–30). He is just and merciful (Rom. 2:6; Lk. 15:1–31). Christian doctrine teaches that God's providence extends to the very least of individual, existing things. In this, it contrasts with the speculations about providence which we find in Averroes and in deists like Voltaire. It is also essentially different both from Muslim fatalism and from Calvinist pessimism.

---

17 Emanationism conceives the world as something which comes forth from the divinity by necessity, sometimes through one or more intermediaries.

Does the excellence of Christian doctrine show its divine origin?

ANTHROPOLOGY. By natural reason we can know that man is endowed with a spiritual and immortal soul, that he is free, and that he is subject to a moral law which depends on God, the supreme law-giver and rewarder. These things are taught by Christian doctrine more clearly than by other religions and by the various systems of philosophy.

The writings which Christians hold to be revealed teach that man is created in the image of God (Gen. 1:26; Wis. 2:23; Eph. 4:24), and that he possesses not only a biological life, which other men can destroy, but also a spiritual soul, which God alone can destroy in hell (Matt. 10:28), and which God calls to glory (Rom. 8:17–18; 2 Tim. 4:8). Man is created to know the true God and to love him above all else, to do his will and to reach eternal life (Jn. 17:3; 1 Tim. 2:4; Matt. 6:21, 33, 25:46).

Anyone who reflects on these Scriptural statements objectively and in good faith ought to be struck both by the way in which they form a unified whole, and by the calm certitude with which they are enunciated. Although, in seeking for the truth, he may find it difficult to prove each of them himself, or to accept the proofs which others have offered, he should nevertheless be able to admit that various Catholic thinkers, by their careful articulation of certain insights common to the human race, have offered what seem like weighty demonstrations of all these assertions. Taken together, these arguments form a body whose salient characteristics, for an honest agnostic, should be its internal consistency, the certitude with which the various truths are proposed, and what we might call a kind of 'intellectual magnanimity'.

Such a person would be in a good position to acquire certainty about the credibility of the Christian religion, for two reasons. First of all, he will notice that these statements about God and man complete the teachings of ancient philosophy, or at least that they are a coherent continuation of those teachings:

CHRISTIANITY IS CREDIBLE

Christian thinkers from the first confronted the problem of the relationship between faith and philosophy, viewing it comprehensively with both its positive aspects and its limitations. [...] They succeeded in disclosing completely all that remained implicit and preliminary in the thinking of the great philosophers of antiquity. The task of these latter [...] was to show how reason, freed from external constraints, could find its way out of the blind alley of myth and open itself to the transcendent in a more appropriate way. Purified and upright, therefore, reason could rise to the higher planes of thought, providing a solid foundation for the perception of being, of the transcendent and of the absolute.[18]

Secondly, our searcher after truth could compare all these Christian doctrines, which are held by a vast number of people of all kinds and all intellectual levels, with the uncertainties and hesitations which have beset even the noblest philosophical endeavours. Even the greatest of Greek thinkers showed themselves unsure when it came to the unicity and personality of God, the creation of the world from nothing, the divine providence exercised over even the least of things, and the personal immortality of the soul. By contrast, since the coming of Christ, hundreds of millions of human beings of all kinds have believed and professed all these essential truths with an entire certainty. The common doctor observes rather poignantly:

> Before the coming of Christ, no philosopher, for all his efforts, was able to know as much about God and the truths necessary for eternal life as one little old woman (*vetula*) can know since the coming of Christ by means of faith.[19]

An enquirer ought to feel that all this constitutes a 'moral miracle', which corroborates what the Catholic magisterium has said on this very subject:

> It is to be ascribed to this divine revelation, that such truths about divine things as of themselves are not

---

18 St John Paul II, encyclical letter *Fides et Ratio*, 41.
19 St Thomas Aquinas, *Commentary on the Creed*, prologue.

beyond human reason, can, even in the present condition of mankind, be known by everyone with facility, with firm assurance, and with no admixture of error.[20]

B. *Supernatural* mysteries

The Christian faith includes mysteries which are intrinsically 'supernatural': these are the Trinity, the Incarnation, and others which are connected to these two. Catholic doctrine states that supernatural mysteries surpass the natural powers of reason, and hence involve reason in a kind of darkness. Yet these mysteries are also "the light of life" (Jn. 8:12), insofar as they are in harmony with what we can know of God naturally, and also with man's own deepest aspirations, even though they require him to struggle against everything within himself that is disordered, especially pride and sensuality.

One of the fundamental tasks of theology is to show that these mysteries imply no contradictions:

> [For truths that surpass reason], our intention should not be to convince our adversary by arguments: it should be *to answer his arguments against the truth*; for, as we have shown, natural reason cannot be contrary to the truth of faith. The sole way to overcome an adversary of divine truth is from the authority of Scripture, which is an authority divinely confirmed by miracles. For that which is above human reason we believe only because God has revealed it. [...] Then, in order to follow a development from the more to the less manifest, we shall proceed to make known this truth which surpasses reason, *answering the objections of its adversaries* and setting forth the truth of faith by probable arguments and by authorities, to the best of our ability.[21]

---

20 1st Vatican Council, DS 3005, quoted in CCC 38.
21 St Thomas Aquinas, SCG, book 1, ch. 9. Cf. the same author's work *On Boethius, concerning the Trinity* q. 2, a. 3, corpus: "In sacred doctrine [theology], we can use philosophy in three ways. First, we use it to demonstrate the truths that precede the faith, and which need to be known in the science of the faith, for example those which are proved about God by natural arguments, such as 'God exists'. [...] Secondly, we use philosophy to understand the truths of the faith with the help of various comparisons, as St Augustine does in his books on

CHRISTIANITY IS CREDIBLE

Theology also sets forth the 'reasons of fittingness' which these mysteries exhibit. Such reasons are found in the analogies which these mysteries have to the natural world, in the harmonious relation of these mysteries to each other, and in their relation to our final end:

> Reason, indeed, enlightened by faith, when it seeks earnestly, piously, and calmly, attains by a gift from God some understanding of mysteries, and that a very fruitful one; partly from the analogy of these mysteries to those things which it naturally knows, and partly from the relations which the mysteries bear to one another and to the last end of man; but reason never becomes capable of apprehending mysteries as it does those truths which constitute its proper object. For the divine mysteries by their own nature so far transcend the created intelligence that, even when delivered by revelation and received by faith, they remain covered with the veil of faith, and shrouded in a certain degree of darkness, so long as we are pilgrims in this mortal life, not yet with God; 'for we walk by faith and not by sight.'[22]

This search for the *harmony* between the supernatural mysteries and what reason can know by nature is a distinctive characteristic of Christian thought, especially compared to Islam. It arises from our duty both to respect the human intellect, naturally directed as it is toward the truth, and also to recognise the unity of God's plan, in which the supernatural order does not only not contradict the order of nature, but also resembles it to a certain extent, insofar as both have the same divine author:

> Ever since St Paul's visit to the Areopagus, Christianity appears before the world with the claim of being the *religio vera* [the true religion]. What this means is that the Christian faith is not based either on poetry or on

---

the Trinity, where he uses many comparisons drawn from philosophical teachings. Thirdly, we use philosophy *to refute arguments put forward against the faith*, either showing that they are false, or showing that they do not prove their conclusion of necessity."

[22] First Vatican Council, DS 3016; the CCC refers to this is para. 90 and 498.

politics—those two great sources of religion. It is based, rather, on knowledge. It worships the Being who is the foundation of all that exists, the 'true God'. With the coming of Christianity, rationality is no longer the enemy of religion; it is itself religion. [...] We can say that the power which made Christianity into a world religion was its synthesis of reason, faith and life. The phrase *religio vera*, in fact, sums up this very synthesis. [...] Today, as in the past, the Christian faith is the choice which gives priority to reason and to what is rational.[23]

For a person who is outside the faith but who studies the question in an unprejudiced way, all this powerfully tends to suggest the truth of Christianity, and to create in him the sense of being in the presence of a certain 'intellectual beauty'. Thus does he come to the very threshold of the mystery.

C. Christian law and Christian life

PRINCIPLE OF ACTION AND PRE-EMINENT GOAL. The law that governs Christian behaviour is noteworthy for its perfection, considered both as a principle of action and in the goal which it sets before us. As a principle of action, that is, as the source of Christian life, it is called the 'law of grace'. "The new Law is principally the grace of the Holy Spirit given to those who believe in Christ."[24] Its aim is perfection: "Be perfect, as your heavenly Father is perfect" (Matt. 5:48). A disciple of Christ must do everything out of love for God, and there can be no higher motive than this. The whole of the Christian life must derive from love:

> One of them, a doctor of the law, asking him, tempting him: Master, which is the greatest commandment in the law? Jesus said to him: Thou shalt love the Lord thy God with thy whole heart, and with thy whole soul, and with thy whole mind. This is the greatest and the first commandment. And the second is like to this:

---

23 Joseph Ratzinger, 'Verité du christianisme', a lecture given at the Sorbonne, on 27th November 1999, re-produced in *La Documentation catholique*, 2nd January, 2007, no. 2217, pp. 31, 33 and 35.
24 St Thomas Aquinas, STh 1a 2ae, 106, 1.

Thou shalt love thy neighbour as thyself. On these two commandments depend the whole law and the prophets (Matt. 22:35–40).

The new law, which Jesus announced, can therefore be called a 'law of love'. It includes all the precepts of natural morality, but they are to be followed from a motive higher than fear, namely, the love of virtue. The precepts of the new Law thereby surpass those of the old covenant. Yet this love of virtue is itself infused and transfigured by the love of *God*, and in this way surpasses the ancient philosophers' ideal of 'excellence by virtue', noble as that ideal was:

> Those who possess virtue are inclined to do virtuous deeds through love of virtue, not on account of some extrinsic punishment or reward. Hence, the new law, which derives its pre-eminence from the spiritual grace instilled in our hearts, is called the 'law of love'. It is described as containing spiritual and eternal promises, which are objects of the virtues, and chiefly of charity. Accordingly, such persons are inclined of themselves to these objects, not as to something foreign but as to something belonging to themselves.[25]

The following remark on the subject of equanimity, or 'peace of soul', is relevant here:

> The most enlightened pagans sought to keep their soul superior to all chance accidents, since they held that the soul was divine in nature. But since we know that the soul is the temple of the Blessed Trinity, should not we enter more often into this sanctuary where God dwells, thereby finding peace, confidence, and new strength? This is the true meaning of that interior life of which the best of the ancient pagans had but a glimmering.[26]

AN ETHICS OF HAPPINESS. "The Sermon on the Mount contains the whole pattern of the Christian life".[27] It is

---

[25] Ibid. 107, 1 ad 2.
[26] Dom Gérard Calvet, *Benedictus*, volume III, *Lettres aux oblats*, Éditions Sainte-Madeleine, Le Barroux, 2011, p. 161.
[27] St Thomas Aquinas, STh 1a 2ae 108, 3.

impossible to read this 'inaugural speech' of the new covenant and to remain unmoved. It begins with an exordium on happiness, because the righteousness of the gospel is an 'ethics of happiness'. It is a righteousness which brings man into an interior and eternal kingdom, but which at the same time exercises its influence externally, in this world of time, upon a person's whole self, and upon the whole of mankind. Charity is as it were the soul of this righteousness, while its body is the keeping of the commandments and the counsels. "Just as the Sermon on the Mount is the summary of the whole of Christian doctrine, so the eight beatitudes are the summary of the whole of the Sermon on the Mount".[28]

Many non-Christians have felt a fascination for the ethical principles advocated by Christianity, especially as they may be seen in the life of Christ himself. Such people thus bear witness to the perfection of these principles. For example, Ernest Renan[29] was an apostate from Catholicism, but the veneration in which he held the person and ethical teaching of Jesus Christ is well known. But this same ethical teaching is admired also by followers of Eastern philosophies and religions, as well as by Jews, Muslims and agnostics. It is true that this admiration is sometimes bound up with confused forms of syncretism, or with attempts to claim Christ in support of some non-Christian ideology or other, yet it is fundamentally a genuine, human response. Here, for example, is the testimony of Abd-el-Jalil, a Muslim from Morocco who later converted and became a Catholic and a religious:

> My reading led me to a second conclusion, namely, that Christianity was, I felt sure, superior in two regards to the religion which I had been practising: in its moral teaching, and in the holiness of its founder. If that was correct, then, provided one accepts the existence of a

---

28 Bossuet, *Méditations sur l'Évangile*, 'Sermon de Notre-Seigneur sur la montagne', 1st day, ŒC, vol. 6, p. 8.

29 Ernest Renan (1823–1892) was a rationalist French author. His 1863 work, *Vie de Jésus*, which was written with considerable skill from a wholly naturalistic perspective, had a great influence in its day.

personal God who possesses all perfection, *it seemed to me impossible that he should have allowed something so beautiful as Catholicism to exist, were it false.* That would be contrary to his wisdom, his goodness, and his justice.[30]

A UNION OF CONTEMPLATION AND ACTION. Christian ethics, as we have seen, both includes and transcends the natural law. It also appears to be uniquely successful in effecting a close union between mystical contemplation and external action. The Jewish philosopher Henri Bergson, who made a lengthy study of this question, considered that Greek, Hindu and Buddhist mysticism were all, by contrast, closed in on themselves, and thus incomplete, because of their lack of such a bond between action and contemplation:

> Only with the great Christian mystics do we find a mysticism which is *complete*. [...] They achieved a degree of vitality from which an extraordinary energy and boldness emerged, along with extraordinary powers of planning and realisation. [...] There is such a thing as [...] a well-rooted and exceptional intellectual sanity, which is easy to recognise. It may be known by these marks: a readiness for action, joined with a capacity constantly to adapt oneself to changing circumstances; a combination of strength and flexibility; and a simplicity of spirit that prevails over the complexities of life. It is a kind of 'higher common sense'. Do we not find exactly this in the lives of these mystics of whom we are speaking? [...] The love which consumes [the Christian mystics] is no longer simply the love of a man for God, but the love of God for all men. Through God and by God he loves mankind with a divine love. This is something other than the 'feeling of brotherhood' which the philosophers have recommended to us in the name of reason. [...] Given that our everyday experience hardly yields the belief that all men share some higher nature, would the philosophers themselves have maintained this belief

---

30 *Mulla-Zadé et Abd-el-Jalil, deux frères en conversion, Du Coran à Jésus, Correspondance 1927–1957*, par Maurice Borrmans, Paris, Le Cerf, 2009, p. 16.

so confidently, were it not for the existence of mystics who have embraced all mankind in a single, indivisible love? [...] One may [...] well wonder whether [Christian mysticism] has ever done anything other than to write out the dogmas of Christianity, but in letters of fire.[31]

D. A sublime harmony

'Sublimity' means beauty that results from the intimate union of things that are diverse. The Trinity is, eminently, sublime, since both communion and personality are present in it to the highest degree. Christ is sublime, since divine nature and human nature, things extremely distant from each other, are united in him in the most intimate way, namely, in his own person. Likewise, Christian doctrine is sublime, because it derives from these two mysteries.

Let us summarise Christian doctrine briefly. It concerns, first of all, God in himself: the eastern Fathers of the Church refer to reflexion on this aspect of the mystery as 'theology'. Secondly, Christian doctrine concerns God's external action: reflexion on this aspect of the mystery is called 'economy'. Christian revelation teaches that God created the world freely, and that by raising man to a supernatural level, God offered him the gift of sharing his own happiness. When man had misused his freedom, according to the doctrine of original sin, God the Son became incarnate to save him, and founded the Church, with its hierarchical and sacramental structure, to bring this redemption to him. By the sending of the Holy Ghost, the Trinity dwells in the souls of the just, and bestows on them sanctifying grace, from which flow the infused virtues, both moral and theological. These virtues give rise to the communion of saints and are a beginning of eternal life, where God is seen by his chosen

---

31 Henri Bergson, *Les deux sources de la morale et de la religion*, Paris, Presses universitaires de Frances, 1962, pp. 240–51. The author refers explicitly to St Paul, St Theresa, St Catherine of Siena, St Francis of Assisi, and St Joan of Arc. His verdict is all the more weighty in that he states that he is "abstracting, for the moment, from their Christianity" (p. 240).

ones face-to-face, and loved by them with all their powers of love, and thus is all in all.

This wonderful divine action can be represented schematically, to show its two movements, one descending and one ascending.[32]

	Trinity	
Creation/elevation		Eternal life
Original Sin		Communion of Saints
Incarnation		Charity
Redemption		Faith/Hope
Church		Grace
Eucharist		Mission of the Holy Spirit

(descending arrow on left, ascending arrow on right)

II. CHRISTIAN DOCTRINE FULFILS MAN'S ASPIRATIONS

A. Christian doctrine satisfies the mind

Non-Christians are sometimes amazed by certain aspects of the wisdom of Christianity, especially by its knowledge of human nature. Malik Bezouh, a former member of the Muslim brotherhood, wrote as follows:

> I came then across a passage of Bossuet's. It was quite an experience! It was my first real contact with French literature. Previously I had read only Islamist translations from Arabic, and now I was reading the Bishop of Meaux's magnificent French prose. I fell in love with his writing, especially with his descriptions of human nature. For example, I was very much taken with what he said about man's feverish concern for appearances: "Ah, when shall I stop trying to appear to be something, whether to others or to myself, and aim simply to *be* it?" That is such a deep thought, and it shows up our own hedonistic and narcissistic society for what it is. It was like a revolution for me, when I came across this great man: a Christian and a Frenchman, a man who was keenly aware of God's transcendence, and who belonged to an age of which I knew nothing. I started

---

32 Cf. Réginald Garrigou-Lagrange, *De Revelatione per Ecclesiam catholicam proposita*, Paris, Lethielleux, 1962, p. 486.

reading all I could about French history, in order to understand Bossuet and the *Ancien Régime*. For me, that felt like finding salvation, or like being born again. All the time this jewel, this treasure, had been in my reach, and I hadn't known it. Bossuet opened a door for me on to the whole wonderful world of French civilisation, and therefore of Christian civilisation too.[33]

Christian wisdom offers not only a perceptive analysis of human nature, but also a far-reaching account of the problems that touch man most nearly: the nature of God, the origin of the world and of man himself, the meaning of life, and our mysterious and distressing tendency to go wrong. The beauty of all this can be appreciated both by a great genius like St Augustine of Hippo and also by simple people, like the *vetula*, or 'little old woman', mentioned above by St Thomas.

Doubtless, Christian wisdom does not do away with all difficulties or mental puzzles. Yet none of the human sciences does this either; this is simply a sign that reality surpasses man's powers of comprehension. Living at a time when general relativity and quantum mechanics have deprived mathematical, physical sciences of their strict determinism, we are better placed than were the 18th and 19th century rationalists to see that 'obscurity' is not synonymous with falsehood. A telling instance of this is the reply that Albert Einstein gave to a Dominican who asked him what he thought about the central mysteries of the Catholic faith:

> We're standing on the middle of the ladder. We're not right at the bottom, since we have emerged from an animal existence. But we are also a long way off the top, since there are many beings who are more intelligent than us. We can't set a limit to the possibilities which matter contains within itself; still less can we set a limit to the power of spirit. And anyway, can we really separate matter from spirit? *As far as I am concerned, none of the mysteries which you tell me about is in any*

---

33   *Famille chrétienne*, n. 1982, 30th December, 2015.

way absurd, and they are much more than just symbols. I am sure that they are realities, but that they have infinitely more meaning than we are able to imagine.[34]

Despite the questions which it leaves unresolved, Christian teaching forms a harmonious whole, with a unique power to touch the heart of anyone willing to consider it without prejudice. Fr Guérard des Lauriers wrote as follows:

> We should not [...] forget that there exists "a light that enlightens every man who comes into the world" (Jn. 1:9). This predisposes anyone of good will to welcome the whole truth. Divine truth can never become *obvious*, not even for the believer, and the propositions which express it may sound strange to someone without faith. Yet it has *an internal consistency*, which makes it its own best apologetic. This internal consistency *cannot fail to influence an honest person, and to exercise its sway over him, for it is deeply attractive to the human mind.* A man's 'feel for truth' is of course greatly increased by the gift of faith. His intellect begins then to live in quite a new atmosphere, as regards its awareness of the reality of divine things, and yet he does not experience this as an imposition on his freedom or as a mere obligation, but rather as a gift: the magnificent fulfilment of every man's eternal vocation to the truth.[35]

A great Jesuit theologian of the last century provides a moving example of this:

> It is not at all unheard of for souls to be won for the Christian faith without any direct, personal contact with preachers of the gospel, but by simply coming into contact with the truths of faith. A classic example of this is the origin of the church in Korea. In the 17th century, some books explaining the faith and morality of Christians were imported to Korea from China, and these were enough to convince a small group of scholars about the gospel. The faith was thus first implanted

---

34 R.-L. Bruckberger, *Au diable le Père Bruck. Mémoires III, L'Amérique, 1950–58*, Paris, Plon, 1986, p. 189.
35 Michel-Louis Guérard des Lauriers, *Les dimensions de la foi*, p. 334 (italics added).

before the arrival of the first missionaries, thanks to the witness which the divine message bore to its heavenly origin, simply by its content.[36]

In our days, those who receive people from Muslim backgrounds into the Church sometimes tell us of conversions which precede preaching of any kind, and which arise from the reading of the synoptic gospels, or the gospel of St John.[37]

B. Christian doctrine attracts the human will

The desire to love God, the hope of achieving blessedness, and the power to love our neighbour and to practise virtue, are all things which appeal to the human will; and they are given to us in Christ. The beginnings of happiness are experienced even in this life, as the visible joy of converts often testifies. This is part of the 'hundred-fold' promised by Christ, and it consists above all in the joy and peace which are fruits of the Holy Spirit, and which are the first, inward effects of charity. Here is a fine passage from the 2nd century, taken from an *apologia* for Christianity written for pagans of good faith. It is the most ancient example of this genre:

> If you, also, ardently desire this faith, and embrace it, then you will begin to know the Father. For God has loved mankind: he created the world for them; he has subjected to them all that is on the earth; he gave them reason and understanding; he granted to them alone to look upward, toward heaven; he formed them to his own image; he sent to them his only-begotten Son; he has promised to them a kingdom in heaven, and he will give it to those who have loved him. And when you shall have known him, what joy, think you, will fill your heart? How will you love him who has first so loved you! By loving him, you will imitate his goodness.

---

36 Guy de Broglio, *Les signes de crédibilité de la révélation chrétienne*, « Je sais — Je crois », Paris, Fayard, 1964, p. 53.
37 See, for example, Mark A. Gabriel, *Jésus et Mahomet*, Romanel-sur-Lausanne, Ourania, 2009; Joseph Fadelle, *Le prix à payer*, Paris, Éditions de l'Œuvre, 2010; Moh-Christophe, Bilek, *Des musulmans qui deviennent chrétiens. Signe des temps pour l'Église*, Éditions Qabel 2013.

CHRISTIANITY IS CREDIBLE

> Do not marvel that a man may imitate God. He can, if God so wills it.[38]

Man's deepest desires derive both from the condition in which he finds himself, and from his capacity for what is infinite. Christianity's remarkable ability to fulfil the aspirations of the human heart seems to depend on the harmony between these desires and the main Christian mysteries. For in passing from the 'economy' of the redemption to the 'theology' of the Trinity, we encounter three aspects of Christian revelation which fulfil a deep human need, while at the same time infinitely surpassing man's expectations: the mysteries of salvation, of the incarnation, and of the undivided Trinity.

First, the mystery of salvation. Human beings experience much mental pain. They feel it when they encounter evil, under its different forms, especially when they see injustice, or when they think of the inescapability of death and the uncertainty of what lies beyond. They yearn to be free of this suffering; and the sharing of the good news teaches them that the cross and resurrection of Christ have defeated the absurdity of existence. It teaches them that happiness is possible, that the good who persevere will be rewarded, and that the evil who are obstinate will be punished.

Next, human beings desire to be loved, supported, and guided. This desire is satisfied, beyond all expectation, by the overwhelming revelation—felt so keenly, for example, by converts from Islam—of God as Love; by the divine Fatherhood and the unfathomable mystery of the gift of the Son. The incarnation of the Son gives them a friend who is both like them in all things, except sin, and also infinitely able to help, since infinitely above them. The sending of the Holy Ghost and the mystery of the Church, along with the inward inspirations which he gives by means of the gifts, and the outward teachings and insights provided by the holy doctors and the Catholic magisterium, produce hope

---

38 *Letter to Diognetus*, 10:1–4.

and confidence. The Beloved is present, he who is provident and infinitely wise.

Finally, love always dreams of a communion which will not do away with distinction. This is ineffably fulfilled by the holy and life-giving Trinity, which we contemplate and love, and in which we participate. For each divine Person is himself in his relation with the others and in his abiding in the divine Essence.

C. Christian doctrine gives birth to a civilisation in which man's whole nature finds fruition

Christianity is the religion of an *incarnate* God. By his holy humanity, Jesus of Nazareth, the perfect image of the invisible God, has brought about a marvellous development of all the various branches of art. He is the true Icon, who came to live among us, and he is the cause of immense advances in painting, sculpture, architecture, and song. People of every country and religion, and of every cultural level, admire the great monuments of Christian art and travel in order to see them. Christian worship, provided it remains true to itself and keeps its sacral character, opens a window upon heaven, from our world of shadows. Its splendour and mysteriousness are evocative of another world, in a way that non-Christians often find fascinating, and which has prompted many conversions. Among many other examples, I shall mention just that of Paul Claudel. Listening to Vespers in the cathedral of Notre Dame one Christmas eve, he was suddenly converted by an overwhelming sense of 'the innocence of God':

> The choir-boys, in their white robes, along with the pupils from the minor seminary of St Nicholas de Chardonnet, were singing something: I would learn later that it was the *Magnificat*. I was standing in the congregation, near the second pillar by the entrance to the choir, on the right-hand side, where the sacristy is. It was then that the event took place which has been the most important thing in my whole life. All at once, my heart was changed, and I believed. I believed with

CHRISTIANITY IS CREDIBLE

entire firmness; I was completely taken out of myself. I believed with so powerful a conviction and with such certainty, free from the least doubt of any kind, that since then, nothing has ever been able to shake my faith, or even to touch it, neither books, nor arguments, nor any of the chance events of a full and busy life. What I experienced, all at once, was a sense of the innocence of God—his eternal 'childhood'. The revelation was overwhelming, something not to be put into words. In that one moment, my heart was changed, and I believed.[39]

For her part, Simone Weil wrote these profound words:

Beauty is the mark of a sort of incarnation of God in the world. The beauty which we experience serves as a proof that the incarnation is possible. [...] A snatch of plain-song may speak as eloquently as a martyr's death. [...] An evil man may have an intense love for music, but I would find it hard to believe that he could thirst after Gregorian chant.[40]

This is a vast subject, about which much has been said. We may consider in particular the case of music. The bodily and 'cosmic' character of Christianity enables human being to 'pray in beauty', to use St Pius X's expression. Christian art makes us see the things of the world truly, in the light of God, who creates them from love. In this way, it gives a 'voice' to all these things. This is why the 'great music of the west' sprang up within the cultural context of Christianity:

St Bernard [...] indicates here that the chant depends upon a true vision of reality. By their prayer and their chant, monks must live up to the greatness of that Word which has been entrusted to them, and which calls, decidedly, for beauty. *This all-important duty of speaking with God, and of singing of him in words which he himself has provided, gave birth to the great music of the west.* This music did not arise out of the kind of personal 'creativity' by which an individual attempts

---

39 Cf. Paul Claudel, *Contacts et circonstances, Œuvres en Prose*, Gallimard, La Pléiade, pp. 1009–10.
40 Simone Weil, *La pesanteur et la grâce*, Plon, 1988, pp. 171–72.

above all to express his own personality, and to set up some monument to himself. It happened, rather, because they sought to listen with the 'ears of the heart', so as to hear the laws which are embedded, so to say, within the musical harmonies of creation, and to recognise the true nature of this music which the Creator has placed within the world, and within man. Then they were able themselves to invent a music which would be worthy of God, and at the time, genuinely worthy of man, and which would clearly manifest man's true worth.[41]

III. THE PERFECTION OF CHRISTIAN TEACHING SUPPORTS ITS DIVINE ORIGIN

The human condition makes it hard to discover the truth. Nevertheless, it is a fact that certain people, the Christians, are able to know the natural law in its entirety and to profess the truth of a sublime and pure religion, despite the difficulties which they experience in practising it. It seems hardly possible to account for this fact by merely natural causes, and so the most plausible explanation is that God is responsible for it.

This argument is, admittedly, not the most immediate means to establish the credibility of Christianity, since it presupposes both a certain familiarity with the whole of Christian doctrine, and also that a person has compared Christianity with other religions and philosophies. However, once the so-called 'external criteria' of prophecy and miracles are in place, this argument from the perfection of Christian doctrine is a valuable one. It can help someone who is seeking the truth in good faith to come to a conclusion, or else it can strengthen a conclusion that he has already reached.

A contemporary theologian has argued along these same lines:

> If God exists but Christianity is only a human invention, this means that man's intellect is more inventive than

---

41 Benedict XVI, *Discours au monde de la culture*, Collège des Bernardins, Paris, 12th September, 2008.

CHRISTIANITY IS CREDIBLE

God's. For, on this view, we have thought of a most wise way for God to act and to save mankind, which has supposedly never occurred to the Creator himself, the eternal Wisdom. Or again, if God exists but Christ is only a human creation and not a messenger from God, then man's heart and man's love are richer and more resourceful than God's; for on this view, the Father of men is less generous than his creatures had supposed him to be. [...]

You may object that the fact that human beings have devised some extravagant fairy-tale and attributed it to God does not mean that he is obliged to carry it out or else be less divine than man. That is true, which is why *the argument just put forward, and which I consider a powerful one, cannot be separated from the earlier arguments*, which established how the whole life of Jesus makes perfect sense; nor, especially, can it be separated from the considerations which I shall offer about the historicity of the Christian revelation.[42]

Fr Guy de Broglie S. J., who also speaks of the excellence of Christian doctrine as an important criterion of credibility, rightly emphasises the need for the correct dispositions on the part of the person who is seeking the truth:

> Earlier apologetics consistently attributed a great value to the *intrinsic* signs of divine authenticity which appear in Christianity: witness the writings of the first patristic apologists, such as the *Letter to Diognetus*, where this kind of argument clearly plays a role of the first importance. Witness also the whole of St Thomas's *Summa contra Gentiles*. The main aim of this latter work seems to be to make known both to non-believers of every kind, and to Christians tempted to abandon their faith, the eminent 'credibility' of a teaching so entirely in harmony with all the highest ideas and aspirations of the human mind. [...] A person may need first to possess a certain sympathy and affinity for Christian teaching in order to be able to grasp it in its entirety and, especially, to appreciate it at its true value. [...] The message of the gospel does objectively possess those marks of excellence

---

42 André Léonard, *Les raisons de croire*, pp. 142–43 (italics added).

which ought to make apparent that it greatly surpasses all that human beings can invent. These marks of excellence are a sufficient foundation for faith, at least for well-disposed and perceptive souls. However, just as the qualities of a painting, for all their objectivity, do not do away with the need for the man who judges it to possess a certain artistic sense, so also, however thoroughly objective a given sign of credibility may be, it will not dispense those who are to judge it from the need to have a certain 'connaturality' with divine things, or at least the beginnings of such a connaturality.[43]

René de Chateaubriand closed his well-known work *Génie du Christianisme* with some lapidary phrases which, while needing to be understood correctly, express a deep truth. That celebrated author ended his long investigation into culture and history as follows:

Christianity is perfect, while men are imperfect.
But a perfect effect cannot derive from an imperfect source.
Therefore Christianity did not come from men.
If Christianity did not come from men, it can have come only from God.
If it came from God, men could have known it only by revelation.
Therefore Christianity is a revealed religion.[44]

We should understand this final statement as expressing a certitude of *rational credibility*; faith itself in Christian revelation cannot be the conclusion of a syllogism. For in order to pass from the statement, "I am sure, on account of these signs, that Christian doctrine is *worthy to be believed* as revealed by God", to the statement, "I believe Christian

---

43   Guy de Broglie, *Les signes de crédibilité...*, pp. 56–57. The knowledge by connaturality of which he speaks is particularly necessary for all those who are seeking to discover new truths; it is what helps them to ask the right questions. Cf. L.-M. de Blignières, *Le mystère de l'être*, Paris, « Bibliothèque Thomiste », Vrin, 2007, pp. 69–84 : « Analyse de l'activité de découverte ».
44   Chateaubriand, *Le genie du christianisme*, NRF-Gallimard, « Bibliothèque de la Pléiade », Paris, 1978, p. 1093.

doctrine as revealed by God", supernatural assistance is necessary, on account of the supernatural character of the object to which our mind must adhere. This assistance is the grace of theological faith.

CHAPTER 5

Is the resurrection of Christ a proof of Christianity?

IN THIS CHAPTER, I SHALL FIRST OF ALL examine the Scriptural evidence which establishes the resurrection of Christ as the basis of Christianity. We shall see that Jesus prophesied his resurrection, that he really died, and that the canonical gospels and the apostles testify that he was seen alive once more. Next, I shall consider the value of those signs which prove the resurrection. Finally, I shall show how the resurrection distinguishes Christianity in an important way from all other religions and philosophies.

I. THE GLORIOUS RESURRECTION OF JESUS OF NAZARETH IS THE FOUNDATION OF CHRISTIANITY

A. *Jesus foretold his resurrection "on the third day"*

The biblical expression, 'on the third day', is to be taken in a broad sense: it was a traditional, rather than mathematically exact, way of expressing a short but sufficient period of time. The 'third day' suggests a process which has run its course and can thus give place to something new. On several occasions, Jesus of Nazareth foretold both his death and also his resurrection 'on the third day'. Twice he foretold it by means of mysterious symbols, preparing those who were well disposed for what was to happen, while preventing those who were already hardening their hearts from falling further into blindness. On the first occasion, he used the symbol of the Temple that would be re-built.

> The Jews, therefore, answered, and said to him: "What sign dost thou shew unto us, seeing thou dost these things?" Jesus answered, and said to them: "Destroy this temple, and in three days I will raise it up." The Jews then said: "Six and forty years was this temple in

building; and wilt thou raise it up in three days?" But he spoke of the temple of his body. When therefore he was risen again from the dead, his disciples rememberedthat he had said this, and they believed the scripture, and the word that Jesus had said (Jn. 2:18–22).

On the second occasion, he spoke of the sign of Jonah.

Then some of the scribes and Pharisees answered him, saying: "Master we would see a sign from thee." Who answering said to them: "An evil and adulterous generation seeketh a sign: and a sign shall not be given it, but the sign of Jonas the prophet. For as Jonas was in the whale's belly three days and three nights: so shall the Son of man be in the heart of the earth three days and three nights" (Matt. 12:38–40).

André Feuillet mentions some interesting details relevant to the literal accuracy of the phrase 'the third day':

> Some of the references to the passion may well display secondary elements. I remarked above that it is only to be expected that a writer's knowledge of what really took place would influence his way of recounting Christ's prophecies. I may mention first of all the phrase "the third day" as showing signs of such influence. We find this phrase three times in Matthew and twice in Luke, while in Mark we find "after three days". It is true that one could argue that the two expressions are equivalent. The expressions "after three days" and "for three days" do not always imply three whole days, either in the Septuagint or in other later Greek authors. They often have the same meaning as "on the third day" [the author gives examples from Gen. 42:17–18; 2 Chron. 10:5, 12; Est. 4:15; 5:1]. Yet despite these examples, it is more likely that Luke and Matthew give us here a correction of the original form, "after three days", which is preserved by Mark. Quite apart from the prediction attributed to Christ by the false witnesses [Matt. 26:61], the form in Mark corresponds to the sign of Jonah of which Christ speaks to the scribes and Pharisees [Matt. 12:40]. Again, the expression "on the third day" was the one hallowed by early Christian tradition when speaking of the resurrection of Christ [the author gives references here to

Is the resurrection of Christ a proof of Christianity?

1 Cor. 15:3–4 and Acts 10:40]. There is thus some reason to suppose that this established phrase [*on the third day*] was substituted for the phrase in the second gospel [*after three days*], the latter being inexact if interpreted literally, since between the death of Jesus and Easter morning, hardly more than one and half days elapsed.[1]

However this may be, Jesus explicitly prophesied his passion and resurrection to his disciples on three occasions. The first was after Peter's confession of faith at Caesarea Philippi: "From that time Jesus began to shew to his disciples that he must go to Jerusalem, and suffer many things from the ancients and scribes and chief priests, and be put to death, and the third day rise again" (Matt. 16:21). The next was after the transfiguration: "When they abode together in Galilee, Jesus said to them: 'The Son of man shall be betrayed into the hands of men, and they shall kill him, and the third day he shall rise again'" (Matt. 17:22–23). The last occasion was during the final journey toward Jerusalem: "Jesus going up to Jerusalem, took the twelve disciples apart, and said to them: 'Behold we go up to Jerusalem, and the Son of man shall be betrayed to the chief priests and the scribes, and they shall condemn him to death, and shall deliver him to the Gentiles to be mocked, and scourged, and crucified, and the third day he shall rise again'" (Matt. 20:17–19).

Christ's enemies themselves knew about this prophecy:

> The next day, which followed the day of preparation, the chief priests and the Pharisees came together to Pilate, saying: "Sir, we have remembered, that that seducer said, while he was yet alive: After three days I will rise again. Command therefore the sepulchre to be guarded until the third day: lest perhaps his disciples come and steal him away, and say to the people: He is risen from the dead; and the last error shall be worse than the first" (Matt. 27:62–64).

---

1 André Feuillet, "Les trois grandes prophéties de la Passion et de la Resurrection des Évangiles synoptiques", *Revue thomiste*, 1962, pp. 537–60; quotation taken from pp. 547–48.

Jesus's enemies were thus well aware that he had spoken of the resurrection as the sign which would fully authenticate his mission.

B. Jesus died in reality, not only in appearance

Different persons and groups bear witness to the death of Jesus. This agreement between the witnesses leaves no room for doubt about whether or not his death is a historical fact.

1. First of all, the four evangelists affirm very clearly that he "expired" (*exepneusen*, Mk. 15:37 and Lk. 23:46), or that he "yielded up his spirit" (*aphèken to pneuma*, Matt. 27:50, *paredôken to pneuma*, Jn. 19:30).

2. The centurion in charge of the soldiers was a direct witness of Jesus's death. He is astonished by the way in which Jesus dies — with enough strength to emit a great cry, and then bowing his head. "The centurion who stood over against him, seeing that crying out in this manner he had given up the ghost, said: 'Indeed this man was the son of God'" (Mk. 15:39).

3. Certain soldiers were charged with putting an end to the lives of the condemned men by breaking their legs; this prevented the crucified person from being able to support himself in order to breathe, and it thus accelerated the dreadful suffocation from which he was dying. All these soldiers recognise that Jesus was already dead:

> The Jews (because it was the parasceve), that the bodies might not remain on the cross on the sabbath day (for that was a great sabbath day), besought Pilate that their legs might be broken, and that they might be taken away. The soldiers therefore came; and they broke the legs of the first, and of the other that was crucified with him. But after they were come to Jesus, when they saw that he was already dead, they did not break his legs (Jn. 19:31–33).

4. The thrust of the lance, performed by one of these executioners, is particularly important in establishing the certainty of death. Roman legionaries used this kind of lance, the *pilum*, to pierce an enemy's heart by passing between

two of his ribs, a manoeuvre which was of necessity lethal. Pierre Barbet, a surgeon who made a careful study of Christ's passion, wrote as follows: "This kind of thrust, to the right-side of the body and reaching to the heart, was *always fatal*. It was a classic move which formed part of the training of the Roman armies. [...] Farabeuf used to teach us that when the thrust was made in the intercostal region, on the *right* side of the sternum, there was no remedy, since this would open the wall of the right auricle, which is extremely thin."[2]

Even if, contrary to historical fact, Jesus had still been alive before this spear-thrust, he would not have survived it. It is an irrefutable proof of the Saviour's death. This is one of the reasons why St John, an eye-witness, was so insistent about it:[3]

> One of the soldiers with a spear opened his side, and immediately there came out blood and water. And he that saw it, hath given testimony, and his testimony is true. And he knoweth that he saith true; that you also may believe. For these things were done, that the scripture might be fulfilled (Jn. 19:34–36).

5. The fact that the chief priests and the Pharisees come to ask Pilate that the tomb be guarded for three days (Matt. 27:62–64), and the way in which they express themselves, prove beyond doubt that they are convinced of the death of their enemy, Jesus of Nazareth. They say: "This impostor said, *while he was alive* [...]", and they are keen that his disciples should not "come and steal him away and say to the people: he is risen *from the dead*". Renan, whom no one will suspect of excessive credulity, wrote as follows:

> The best guarantee which the historian has, in a question of this kind, is the hatred and suspicion of Jesus's enemies. It is very doubtful that the Jews were much afraid, from that moment, that Jesus might appear to

---

2 Pierre Barbet, *La Passion de N.-S. Jésus Christ selon le chirugien*, Paris/Sherbrooke (Québec), 1965, p. 180 (original italics).
3 Other reasons are that it fulfilled the prophecies, and that the blood and water which came forth from Christ's side had a mystical meaning.

have risen again; but they must have been very careful to make sure that he died.[4]

6. The Mother of Jesus, the holy women, and St John were present at the foot of the cross, and they witnessed Jesus as he breathed his last. If the least doubt remained about his death, how could they have allowed him to be buried by Joseph of Arimathea, Nicodemus, and the other devout men who took this task upon themselves, and who were themselves friends of the Master? How, in such a case, could they have watched his body being placed in winding cloths with aromatical spices (Jn. 19:40), and wrapped in a great piece of clean linen (Matt. 27:59; cf. Lk. 23:53, Mk 15:46) without intervening? Moreover, the cloth placed over his face (the *sudarium*) would certainly have suffocated a dying man.

7. Forty days afterwards, Peter addressed a large crowd, among whom were many who had been witnesses of Christ's passion. In two important speeches, he recalls what had happened, and emphasises the active role which his hearers had taken in the dramatic events:

> Ye men of Israel, hear these words: Jesus of Nazareth, a man approved of God among you, by miracles, and wonders, and signs, which God did by him, in the midst of you, as you also know: this same being delivered up, by the determinate counsel and foreknowledge of God, you by the hands of wicked men have crucified and slain; whom God hath raised up, having loosed the sorrows of hell [...] The God of Abraham, and the God of Isaac, and the God of Jacob, the God of our fathers, hath glorified his Son Jesus, whom you indeed delivered up and denied before the face of Pilate, when he judged he should be released. But you denied the Holy One and the just and desired a murderer to be granted unto you. But the author of life you killed, whom God hath raised from the dead, of which we are witnesses (Acts 2:22–24, 3:13–15).

---

4 Ernest Renan, *Vie de Jésus*, ch. 26, « Jésus au tombeau », Paris, NRF, Éditions Gallimard, « Collection Folio », 1974, p. 406.

Those present do not dispute Peter's words in any way, as they would have been strictly obliged to do, as devout Jews, if there had been any trickery about Jesus's death. Rather, very many of them accept Peter's preaching, being "struck to the heart", and they go on to receive baptism (cf. Acts 2:37–41, 4:4).

8. St Paul speaks of the death of Jesus of Nazareth as a public fact, which he himself heard of from eye-witnesses. Around the year 55, hardly more than 25 years after the events, he writes to the Corinthians: "For I delivered unto you first of all, which I also received: how that Christ died for our sins, according to the scriptures" (1 Cor. 15:3). He received this testimony very shortly after the passion: first of all, just after his conversion, in Damascus from Ananias, around the year 35 (cf. Acts 9:10–19); then in Jerusalem from Peter and James, around the year 37 (cf. Gal. 1:18–19).

9. We may also add the following:

> It is historically and psychologically *impossible* for the first Christians to have invented the shameful death of Jesus on the Cross. The horror of this form of execution was still keenly felt during the first century, and the evangelists themselves do not delay over their descriptions of it. The 'criterion of difficulty' is fully in favour of the historicity of the event.[5]

C. Jesus rose again

We possess six documents which speak of the resurrection of Christ. These are separate documents, none of which has a literary dependence on the others, and they all date to the first century. In chronological order, they are 1 Corinthians 15; Matthew 28; Mark 16:1–8; Luke 24; the last part of Mark, 16:9–20; and John 21 and 22. They are all notable for their restraint: none claims to describe the act of resurrection itself (the resurrection *in fieri*). They simply give the testimonies

---

5 Bernard Lucien, *Apologétique. La crédibilité...*, p. 537 (original italics). The 'criterion of difficulty' refers to "actions or words of Jesus which would have placed the early Church in a difficult position", ibid. p. 410.

of those who saw Jesus after he had risen (the resurrection *in facto esse*).

We have seen already that the canonical gospels enjoy all the authority that belongs to historical documents.[6] Unlike the apocryphal gospels, they recount events in a sober fashion. When they speak of the resurrection, they are speaking of an event which is an essential part of their message, and which is consistent with the rest of their teaching. They are thus worthy of belief.

As an example of the style of the apocryphal writings, on the other hand, we may cite the description of the resurrection in the 'Gospel of Peter':

> Now in the night whereon the Lord's day dawned, as the soldiers were keeping guard two by two in every watch, there came a great sound in the heaven, and they saw the heavens opened and two men descend thence, shining with a great light, and drawing near unto the sepulchre. And that stone which had been set on the door rolled away of itself and went back to the side, and the sepulchre was opened and both of the young men entered in. When therefore those soldiers saw that, they waked up the centurion and the elders (for they also were there keeping watch); and while they were yet telling them the things which they had seen, they saw again three men come out of the sepulchre, and two of them sustaining the other and a cross following, after them. And of the two they saw that their heads reached unto heaven, but of him that was led by them that it overpassed the heavens. And they heard a voice out of the heavens saying: "Hast thou preached unto them that sleep?" And an answer was heard from the cross, saying: "Yea." Those men therefore took counsel one with another to go and report these things unto Pilate. And while they yet thought thereabout, again the heavens were opened and a man descended and entered into the tomb.[7]

---

6 Cf. chapter 1.
7 *The Apocryphal New Testament*, M. R. James (trans.), 'The Gospel of Peter', IX–XII/35–45, (Clarendon Press: Oxford, 1924).

Is the resurrection of Christ a proof of Christianity?

It is noteworthy how the apostles never seek to defend the fact of the resurrection: they speak of it with serenity, as something beyond dispute. Another significant fact is that they do not attempt to harmonise apparent contradictions in their accounts. While this makes it difficult to calculate the precise sequence of events on Easter Day,[8] it does refute the suggestion that the evangelists worked out among themselves a common version of the facts.

From the start of their preaching, the apostles testified that the resurrection had really occurred. St Peter declares to the Jews on Pentecost:

> Jesus of Nazareth, a man approved of God among you, by miracles, [...] as you also know [...], you by the hands of wicked men have crucified and slain; whom God hath raised up, having loosed the sorrows of hell [...] This Jesus hath God raised again, whereof all we are witnesses. [...] Therefore let all the house of Israel know most certainly, that God hath made both Lord and Christ, this same Jesus, whom you have crucified (Acts 2:23–24, 32–36).

This is the very heart of the 'kerygma' (the initial preaching of the gospel), and the apostles affirm it with certainty as something of which they themselves are witnesses.

NEITHER FRAUD NOR HALLUCINATION. This testimony is credible. It is a product neither of fraud nor of collective hallucination.

Not fraud. Throughout the gospel, the apostles and disciples show no tendency to invent anything. We might almost go so far as to say that they are rather unimaginative, literal-minded people; for example, their ideas about the Messiah simply correspond to the conceptions that were generally prevalent among the Jews at the time. They are slow to believe the very thing which they are supposed to have invented! Nor would they have been able to invent anything, given the state of panic and demoralisation into

---

8   However, I set out a plausible hypothesis in an appendix.

which the disaster of Christ's passion had put them. The theory of fraud on the part of the disciples has therefore been abandoned today by scholars, even by the rationalists and atheists among them.

Not hallucination.[9] The apostles describe the appearances of Christ after his resurrection as real events. The language which they use is the same as that which they use in describing other realities accessible to the senses, in particular the three preceding resurrections, which were also real: those of the daughter of Jairus, of the widow's son, and of Lazarus. Again, the apostles are together when they see Jesus, and they clearly hear what he says. They touch his wounds. As a further proof, Thomas, the unbelieving disciple, is convinced of the resurrection even without touching Christ's body, simply by seeing him, which shows that Jesus must have had all the appearance of a real person.

The appearances of Christ are many and varied, and they extend over forty days. Yet the apostles, far from being elated and excited, are slow to believe. They do not admit the fact of the resurrection until it has become undeniable. Finally, we should note that afterwards they give their testimony to this fact consistently, in a way that is bold yet calm, as to something which has changed their lives—and will make them liable to lose them.

THE UNIQUE IMPORTANCE OF ST PAUL'S TESTIMONY. St Paul was originally a zealous persecutor of the Christians, being a Pharisee of the strict observance. If the Jews in Judaea had possessed any arguments against the reality of Jesus's resurrection or against the reliability of the witnesses, St Paul would certainly have known them, and his conversion would be entirely implausible.[10]

---

[9] For a useful exposition of ten criteria which distinguish 'states of ordinary consciousness' from the 'states of altered consciousness' characteristic of hallucination, see Bernard Lucien, *Apologétique. La crédibilité...*, p. 545. This makes it clear that the accounts in the gospel cannot be explained scientifically by appealing to such abnormal states.
[10] Bernard Lucien, *Apologétique. La crédibilité...* p, 543.

Is the resurrection of Christ a proof of Christianity?

St Paul bears witness to Jesus's resurrection in the oldest of the New Testament writings, which dates to around the year 51:

> For they themselves [in Macedonia and Achaia] relate of us, what manner of entering in we had unto you; and how you turned to God from idols, to serve the living and true God, and to wait for his Son from heaven (whom he raised up from the dead), Jesus, who hath delivered us from the wrath to come. [...] We will not have you ignorant, brethren, concerning them that are asleep, that you be not sorrowful, even as others who have no hope. For if we believe that Jesus died, and rose again; even so them who have slept through Jesus, will God bring with him (1 Thess. 1:9–10; 4:13–14).

Not long after this, around the year 55, the apostle to the nations speaks of Christ's resurrection as a fact perfectly well known to the Church, and as the cornerstone of the faith:

> I make known unto you, brethren, the gospel which I preached to you [around the year 50], which also you have received, and wherein you stand [...] For I delivered unto you first of all, which I also received [from Ananias around the year 35, and from Peter and James around the year 37]: how that Christ died for our sins, according to the scriptures: and that he was buried, and that he rose again the third day, according to the scriptures: and that he was seen by Cephas; and after that by the eleven. Then he was seen by more than five hundred brethren at once: of whom many remain until this present, and some are fallen asleep. After that, he was seen by James, then by all the apostles. And last of all, he was seen also by me, as by one born out of due time. [...] If Christ be not risen again, then is our preaching vain, and your faith is also vain. Yea, and we are found false witnesses of God: because we have given testimony against God (1 Cor. 15: 1, 3–8, 14–15).

The choice of Matthias to replace Judas confirms that there was a necessary connexion between being an apostle and being a witness to the resurrection. The very definition of an apostle is someone who has *seen* Christ in glory.[11] This is why Peter asserts that they must choose "[one] of these men who have companied with us all the time that the Lord Jesus came in and went out among us, beginning from the baptism of John, until the day wherein he was taken up from us" as being "a witness with us of his resurrection" (Acts 1:21–22).

The rational inference from all this is that the resurrection is historical:

> The mystery of Christ's resurrection is a real event, with manifestations that were historically verified, as the New Testament bears witness. [...] The faith of the first community of believers is based on the witness of certain definite men known to the Christians and for the most part still living among them. [...] Given all these testimonies, Christ's Resurrection cannot be interpreted as something outside the physical order, and it is impossible not to acknowledge it *as an historical fact*. [...] The hypothesis that the Resurrection was produced by the apostles' faith (or credulity) will not hold up. On the contrary their faith in the Resurrection was born, under the action of divine grace, from their direct experience of the reality of the risen Jesus.[12]

II. JESUS "SHOWED BY CLEAR SIGNS THAT HE HAD TRULY RISEN AGAIN"[13]

A. By many proofs

St Luke wrote: "Jesus showed himself [to the apostles] alive after his passion by many proofs (*tekmèria*) for forty days" (Acts 1:3). These proofs established the miracle of the resurrection; they are indubitable 'signs of credibility'.[14] They include the empty tomb, with the unusual arrangement of the burial cloths;[15] the words of the angels who declare

---

11 Cf. 1 Cor. 9:1: "Am I not an apostle? Have I not seen Jesus our Lord?"
12 CCC 209, 639, 642, 643, and 644 (italics added).
13 St Thomas Aquinas, STh, 3a 55, 5.
14 A miracle is an *indirect* proof, by a certain sign, of the doctrine which it attests; cf. chapter 3, section I: "Miracles as proof of doctrine".
15 On this point, see Vittorio Messori, *Ils disent: « Il est ressuscité ». Enquête sur le Tombeau vide,* Paris, François-Xavier de Guibert, 2004,

that the prophecies have been fulfilled; and the appearances of Christ to his friends and disciples, who knew him well, having been in close contact with him for three years. During these appearances, he tells them that he is truly a man. These proofs, "taken together, perfectly manifest the resurrection of Christ".[16]

The body of Jesus. It is real and tangible. It is a human body and is seen by the apostles and recognised by them as the very body that was crucified. "See my hands and my feet, that it is I myself" (Lk. 24:39). On certain occasions, as with the appearances to Mary Magdalene and to the two disciples on the road to Emmaus, he is not immediately recognised. But a moment comes when Jesus causes himself to be recognised, and then they have complete certainty, and they go with entire conviction to tell others that they have seen him.

The soul of Jesus. It can perform the three kinds of activity which belong to a soul: vegetative acts (Jesus eats and drinks); sentient acts (he greets others and responds when they ask him questions); and intellectual acts (he carries on a conversation and expounds the Scriptures). "Beginning at Moses and all the prophets, he expounded to them in all the scriptures, the things that were concerning him" (Lk. 24:27).

B. No demonstration of the mystery as such

These proofs, however, do not constitute a demonstration of the resurrection considered as a *mystery*. This point is important, lest a spurious rationalism distort the true aim of apologetics. The glorious condition of Christ after his resurrection is a supernatural mystery in the strict sense: it is entirely beyond the scope of human reason. Hence, it cannot be made evident in itself. Jesus's appearances give us the certainty that having been dead, he returned to life. In this sense, the miracle of the resurrection is an established

---

chapter XI, « Il vit et il crut » and chapter XII, « Du linceul, du suaire et du bandelette », pp. 123–38.
16   St Thomas, STh 3a 55, 6 ad 1.

historical fact, as we saw above with the quotation from the *Catechism*. Yet Christ did not return to this mortal life; he entered an immortal and glorious life which is a true mystery. The circumstances in which Jesus appeared after his resurrection show that he no longer belonged to the familiar world of our natural, earthly experience. He shows himself only intermittently; he comes (even if the doors are shut) as one who is in a sense 'already there'; he leaves without visible motion, as with the disciples on the road to Emmaus, or in the Upper Room. He causes himself to be recognised, after a period of time in which he was not recognised, as with Mary Magdalene on Easter morning, with the disciples going to Emmaus, and with the apostles when he appears on the shore of Lake Tiberias. All these things indicate that he is in a new state of being. Unlike Lazarus, Jesus has not returned to an ordinary, mortal life. He has entered an immortal life, in which his body, now spiritualised (*sôma pneumatikon*, 1 Cor. 15:44) is entirely an 'epiphany of his soul' and is free and sovereign in relation to the cosmos.

C. This miracle leads well-disposed souls toward the mystery

What is a mystery? It is a hidden reality which surpasses our knowledge and is worthy to be known. God can reveal a mystery, by signs which allow man to know that it is he, the infinitely wise and truthful being, who is speaking. In such a case, one can and should say: "Everything revealed by God is true and should be believed. But through Christ, God has revealed the truths of faith which the Catholic Church teaches, in particular, the resurrection. Therefore the truths of faith taught by the Catholic Church are credible and ought to be believed (by mankind in general)." Faith, however, is not the conclusion of this apologetic syllogism. One must take a further step, in order to say: "This should be believed by *me*, here and now." Under the action of grace, our will can move our intelligence to yield a rational assent to God who reveals himself, with the intelligence itself being raised up at the same time by the infused light of faith.[17] But this act is an intrinsically *supernatural* one, and our will is free to refuse it, since a mystery is never obvious to the human mind. In particular, if our emotions are not well-governed, they are likely to be an obstacle to this act of faith.

"Thomas saw one thing and believed another; he saw the wounds and believed him to be God".[18] The culmination of Jesus's appearances after his resurrection is his charge to the apostolic college to bear witness to the whole world:

> Since Christ rose by a glorious resurrection, this resurrection was not manifested to everyone, but to some, by whose testimony it could be brought to the knowledge of others. [...] The apostles were able to testify to the resurrection even by sight, because from the testimony of their own eyes they saw (*oculata fide viderunt*) Christ alive, whom they had known to be dead.[19]

III. THE RESURRECTION: UNIQUE TO CHRISTIANITY

A. Are there equivalent accounts elsewhere?

Certain works of comparative religion, and certain Modernist writers such as Loisy, have sought to deny the uniqueness of the Christian doctrine of the resurrection of Jesus, true God and true man.[20] They have made it out to be a 'Christian myth', analogous to the myths of other cultures, speaking for example of "the very old story of the dying and rising god", and referring to Osiris, Dionysios-Zagreus, Adonis-Tammouz, and Attis. In the limits of this book, I cannot describe all these myths in detail: instead, I shall quote a Jesuit apologist who made a thorough study of them, and who was well acquainted with the best scholarship in the field of the history of the mystery-religions:

---

17 Cf. CCC 153–56.
18 St Thomas Aquinas, STh, 3a 55, 5 ad 3.
19 Ibid. 55, 1 and 55, 2 ad 1.
20 Alfred Loisy (1857–1940) was a Catholic priest, generally reckoned the founder of the Modernist movement, which attacked the reliability of Scripture. He was excommunicated by Pope St Pius X.

The idea of a god who dies and rises again in order to lead those who believe in him to eternal life is not found in any of the Hellenic mystery-religions. The victory of the god over suffering and death is a *symbol and pledge* for the initiate, who is burdened by the sorrows of earthly life, of a blessed life hereafter. Since the sufferings and death of the god cause the god to resemble him, they give him the hope that he will be fully assimilated to the god's divine condition. But the death of the god is not an expiatory sacrifice. It is not this death which obtains salvation. [...] In fact, the epithet *Sôter* (Saviour) is not at all characteristic of the gods of the mystery-religions and is not bestowed upon them before the Christian era. [...]

It is in any case clear that the roots of the Christian concept of redemption, of *sôtèria,* are to be found not in pagan and Hellenistic precursors, but in the Old Testament and in Judaism. [...] These 'dying and rising' demi-gods do not go through any passion and resurrection, in the traditional sense of those words. Their life is cut short by some tragic accident which they themselves do not intend. Afterwards, they attain some permanent restoration—but the analogy stops there, and if one tries to make anything more of it, it falls apart.

[...] They [the mystery religions] have been grafted as well as possible on to immemorial rituals. They are laborious attempts to solve the problem of man's fate, whether here or beyond the grave; or sometimes they symbolise the rhythm of the seasons, in human imagery [...] The question of whether what was attributed to these gods corresponded to anything that had really happened in the past did not even arise. It did not arise for the simple people, who were edified or excited when they came into contact with these liturgies, the splendour and antiquity of which concealed the horrors that lay at their origins. Nor did it arise for the learned who underwent or exploited these rites. At best, they were entirely a matter of teaching and parables, poetry and myths—that is to say, they were fables.

But it is not only that some modern authors have imposed the Christian framework of 'passion and resurrection' onto the myths and stories of cultures to which it does not belong. There is also an obvious contradiction between, on the one hand, the vagueness which these myths exhibit in their form and content, and on the other, the factual precision of the gospels with their doctrine of the redeeming death of a God who leads his faithful to eternal life.

More specifically, we can say that in the *myths*, what we encounter are demi-gods who personify the various seasons, or else we find the worship of the generative power, with the woman occupying the most prominent place. In the *pagan mysteries*, the essential thing is the rite itself, but understood in a materialistic and magical way, as automatically guaranteeing the survival of the initiate.

As for *re-incarnation* in its various forms (Hinduism, Buddhism, Pythagorean and Platonist philosophy, spiritism, and theosophy), this involves a contempt for matter, something quite absent from Christianity, which is the religion of a God who becomes incarnate. The idea of reincarnation is also based on a mistaken understanding of finite being, seen as a 'part' of the divine Being. These doctrines sometimes belittle the human person, when he or she is taken to be an illusion created by desire. Reincarnation offers no definitive, satisfying answer to the problem of reward and retribution, nor does it offer any doctrine of *salvation*, either for the individual person, or for the world, which is something really distinct from God.

B. Only Christianity offers a 'complete salvation': the resurrection of the dead

"The resurrection of the dead is the faith proper to Christians".[21]

Death is a metaphysical catastrophe. It attacks the very substance of the human being, since matter is a part of his essence: to be dead means *no longer to possess one's nature*, no longer to exist as a person. Death appears to man as the

---

21   St Augustine, *Sermon* 241.1

supreme misfortune; it suggests that human nature is being punished for something, as we know by faith to be true.[22]

Reason by itself can recognise that Christianity is nothing less than an endeavour to confront evil in its entirety, including the evil of death. It is the only religion which sets itself the goal of triumphing completely over evil and death, for the universal good:

> For it became him, for whom are all things, and by whom are all things, who had brought many children into glory, to perfect the author of their salvation, by his passion. For both he that sanctifieth, and they who are sanctified, are all of one. For which cause he is not ashamed to call them brethren, saying: "I will declare thy name to my brethren; in the midst of the church will I praise thee." And again: "I will put my trust in him." And again: "Behold I and my children, whom God hath given me." Therefore because the children are partakers of flesh and blood, he also himself in like manner hath been partaker of the same: that, through death, he might destroy him who had the empire of death, that is to say, the devil: and might deliver them, who through the fear of death were all their lifetime subject to servitude. For no where doth he take hold of the angels: but of the seed of Abraham he taketh hold. Wherefore it behoved him in all things to be made like unto his brethren, that he might become a merciful and faithful priest before God, that he might be a propitiation for the sins of the people. For in that, wherein he himself hath suffered and been tempted, he is able to succour them also that are tempted (Heb. 2:10–18).

While only *faith* can persuade us that Christ's resurrection overcomes all sorrow and misfortune, *reason* can see that this plan of salvation makes perfect sense. Here are some thought-provoking words from a philosopher, which bring out the meaning of this key part of the Christian mystery:

---

22 Cf. St Thomas, SCG, book 4, chapter 52: "Taking into account divine providence, we can reckon it fairly likely that God had [originally] united the higher nature to the lower in order that the former might rule over the latter."

Man dies [...] justly. He is destroyed as to his very essence; this is what makes death so grievous. But the Gospel tells us that a man has died, this time, for no reason: that is, unjustly. Jesus's death lacks the culpability which we have found in other men's, since his human nature is intact. [...] However, Jesus took to himself the reason which we have for dying [...] He entered into solidarity with all human beings in their nature; that is to say, he 'espoused' to himself that which, in their nature, means they must die [...] He made himself 'sin' in order to become 'death'. [...]

For a man without fault to be put to death is once more 'an act without reason', and a double fault. Death, this time, has not been just, for it has struck down an innocent man. This is why he rises again and is reborn from the dead. But since he who died without reason rises again in accord with reason, his rising again means that as a just compensation he brings back to life those whom he found dead in the world below; those who were in solidarity with him in his new birth enter alongside him into life. [...]

Since he died without a reason, unjustly, Jesus, having risen again, is safe from ever having to return to death. Uniting oneself to him means making his cause one's own; it means joining his side. And those who do this will die in such a way that death itself expires, and so they rise to life with him whose cause they chose. [...]

If we exclude this theory, at any rate, we shall find nothing else in history which would be a match for evil and able to save us. If a man did not possess here-and-now this unprecedented, unheard of reason for dying, and so for rising again, he would be forever lost.[23]

Christianity tells us that this is indeed true. It teaches that the baptismal character makes us share in *that which Jesus is*: the Word made flesh (the mystery of the incarnation); a man who accepts death (the mystery of the redemption); and the one who gives the Spirit renewing all things (the mystery of the resurrection).

---

23 Florent Gaboriau, *Nouvelle Initiation Philosophique*, Casterman, 1965, vol. 5, pp. 206–7, 210.

C. Christ's resurrection is a promise of complete beatitude for mankind

Romano Guardini points out how unique the human body is in Christian thought, since it sees the body as in a way divinised by the resurrection:

> At the beginning of the modern era, it was made into a dogma that Christianity is the enemy of the body. But the people who said that were using the word 'body' like pagan antiquity or the Renaissance, or as happens in our own day: the body as separated from God and idolized. In reality, it is only Christianity which has ventured to see the body as one of the greatest secrets of God.[24]

Joseph Ratzinger shows the connection between this doctrine and that of creation:

> Faith in the resurrection of Jesus is a profession of faith in the real existence of God and in his creative act, and in God's entire approval of creation and matter. God's word truly penetrates the depths of the body.[25]

The bodily resurrection of the just will be a fruit of Christ's own resurrection and will make the final blessedness of the saved to be something genuinely complete. Because of the resurrection, we can say with conviction that "all that is assumed (by Christ) is saved."[26] All the elements of the cosmos have been assumed into Christ's glory, and this will redound to the happiness of the saints in their glorious state. The various elements of the saints' beatitude will be superbly ordered among themselves. The *spiritual* elements — the vision of the divine essence; the full knowledge of the truth; the friendship among the elect, both human and angelic; eternity itself — will shed their light upon the *moral* elements: art, virtue and honour. And both the spiritual and the moral

---

[24] R. Guardini, *Le Seigneur*, Alsatia, 1975, vol. 2, p. 126. English version: *The Last Things*, Cluny Media, 2019,.
[25] Joseph Ratzinger, *Le Ressuscité*, DDB, 1986, p. 131.
[26] A corollary of the patristic axiom, "what the Word has not assumed is not saved" (Gregory of Nazianzen, poem *De incarnatione adversus Apollinarium*, PG 37: 466–68).

elements will quicken the material aspect of beatitude, that is, the glorified bodies delighting in the cosmos after its transfiguration:

> The body, then, will be commonly disposed in all men in harmony with the soul, with this result: The incorruptible form bestows an incorruptible being on the body in spite of its composition from contraries, because in respect to corruption the matter of the human body will be entirely subject to the human soul. But the glory and power of the soul elevated to the divine vision will add something more to the body which is united to it. For this body will be entirely subject to the soul — the divine power will effect this — not only in regard to its being, but also in regard to action, passion, movements, and bodily qualities. Therefore, just as the soul which enjoys the divine vision will be filled with a kind of spiritual lightsomeness, so by a certain overflow from the soul to the body, the body will in its own way put on the lightsomeness of glory. Hence, the Apostle says: "It is sown in dishonour. It shall rise in glory." [...] Just as the glory to which the human soul is exalted exceeds the natural power of the heavenly spirits, as was shown in Book III, so does the glory of the risen body exceed the natural perfection of the heavenly bodies, so as to have a greater lightsomeness, a more assured impassibility, a greater freedom of movement, and a higher dignity of nature. [27]

---

[27] St Thomas Aquinas, SCG, book 4, chapter 86, n. 1, 2, 6.

CHAPTER 6

Jesus's self-description: a sign of his divine mission

I. JESUS'S WITNESS ABOUT HIMSELF

Jesus of Nazareth testified to the mystery of his own person. He spoke of himself in three ways: as the *Messiah*; as a *Teacher*, commissioned by God to impart a revelation which all must accept in order to be saved; and *as the Son of God and God himself*. For the sake of brevity, I shall limit myself to considering this last aspect, which is the most important, and which in a way includes the other two: for if Jesus is the true Son of God, we may certainly have confidence in him when he presents himself as Messiah and Teacher:

> The first thing that characterises the person of Jesus is that, both in his words and his deeds, he claimed to be divine. This is wholly unique in human history. Jesus is the only man who, while being in his right mind, has claimed to be equal to God.[1]

Jesus did not only behave like a God, acting with divine authority, stating that he is above every creature, doing that which God alone does in the Old Testament, and claiming to possess God's own power.[2] He also said that he was God.

Jesus first implies, then affirms, his own pre-existence
Jesus implied his own pre-existence by saying on many occasions, "I have *come*". He does this both in the synoptic gospels[3] and in St John: "I have not come of myself, but he that sent me is true" (Jn. 7:28). The phrase "he that sent me"

---

1 André Léonard, *Les raisons de croire*, p. 97.
2 Cf. Louis-Marie de Blignières, *Le mystère du Christ*, Poitiers, DDM, 2013, pp. 35–40.
3 Cf. Matt. 5:17, 10:34, 20:28; Mk. 10:45; Lk. 19:10, 12:49–51.

Jesus's self-description: a sign of his divine mission

occurs twenty-five times in the gospel of St John. So, from where has he come? Pilate's question, "Where are you from?" (Jn. 19:8), that is, "What is your origin—who exactly are you?" is present throughout the Gospel. Both in his conversation with Nicodemus and in his discourse on the Bread of Life, Jesus speaks of his heavenly origin: "I have come down from heaven" (Jn. 6:38; cf. Jn. 3:13).

Did that mean, as Origen supposed, that his soul pre-existed the incarnation and that it had been created with the angels at the beginning of the world? A dramatic conversation between Jesus and the Pharisees (Jn. 8) leads Christ to make an affirmation which excludes a merely temporal pre-existence of that kind. When the Jews attack him for making himself greater than Abraham, saying "Who do you claim to be?", Jesus ranks Abraham himself below the mystery of his own person: "Abraham your father rejoiced that he might see my day; he saw it and was glad."[4] The Jews then say to him: "You are not yet fifty years old, and have you seen Abraham?" At that point, deliberately breaking with the accepted practices of his time, Jesus attributed to himself the mysterious divine name that had been revealed to Moses, *I am* (Ex. 3:14), thus claiming for himself an eternal Personhood. "Amen, amen, I say to you, before Abraham was, *I am*" (Jn. 8:58). Claudio G. Morino observes:

> His *ego sum* [I am], as well as bearing witness to his eternal existence, also proclaims his divinity. For just as the phrase *I am* in the Old Testament is a revelation of the being of God (cf. Ex. 6:6, 7:5; Is. 45:5; Hos. 13:4; Joel 2:27), so in the fourth gospel, the words *I am*, when they occur on the lips of Jesus, are a revelation and affirmation of his divine person.[5]

The Jews understood perfectly well that Jesus was attributing to himself a divine mode of existence, and so they

---

[4] Jesus here applies to himself another phrase that was reserved for God, that of the 'day of the Lord' (cf. Amos 5:18).
[5] Cladio G. Morino, *Verbum Dei semen*, vol. 2, *Identité et mission de Jésus-Christ*, Téqui, Paris, 1983, p. 152.

prepared to administer the penalty reserved for one who has 'blasphemed the name of the Lord' (Lev. 24:16). "They took up stones therefore to cast at him" (Jn. 8:59).

B. Jesus affirms the equality of his knowledge to God's

Two of the synoptic gospels contain a fine pericope[6] expressing a dramatic claim, nothing equivalent to which can be found either in Judaism or in Hellenism: for no one had ever claimed to be the only person to know God. "All things are delivered to me by my Father, and no one knows the Son but the Father. Neither does anyone know the Father, but the Son, and he to whom it shall please the Son to reveal him" (Matt. 11:27). Not only does Jesus declare that he is the only one who possesses and can pass on the secrets of the godhead; he also affirms that no one can know him, Jesus, except God: "No one knows who the Son is, but the Father" (Lk. 10:22).

But who can put the mystery of his own identity on the same level as the mystery of the identity of God? If the Father and Son are equal in their knowability, they must also be equal in their *being,* since God alone can know himself fully. St Irenaeus, who was one of the 'apostolic fathers' and had known the followers of St John, explains:

> Though the Father is invisible for us, he is known by his own Word; though he is inexpressible, he is expressed by the Word. Conversely, the Word is not known except by his Father only. This is the two-fold truth which the Lord has made known to us.[7]

C. Jesus refers to himself as the Son, in a true and mysterious sense

Jesus prepared people to accept this affirmation of himself as the Son, by his manner of teaching and preaching, and by the signs with which he accompanied and authenticated his words (cf. Jn. 15:22–24). For example, he told the parable

---

6   A pericope is a short passage of Holy Scripture.
7   St Irenaeus, *Against the Heresies,* IV.6.

of the Wicked Husbandmen, whose meaning is clear (Mk. 12:1–12). This parable alludes to the prophets, whom God sent to his 'vine', that is, to the chosen people (cf. Is. 5:1–7), but who are rejected and persecuted by them. Then God sends 'his beloved Son', and this son, 'the heir', is put to death like the others by the murderous tenants of the vineyard, only to be raised up by God as the 'key-stone'.

Again, when speaking of the last judgement, Jesus does not disclose the day when it will take place, since, despite his knowledge of all the Father's secrets (cf. Matt. 11:27), it was not part of his mission to do so. Yet he refers to himself as *Son* in a sense which is more than human, since it implies a rank even higher than that of the angels of heaven: "Of that day or hour no one knows, neither the angels in heaven, nor the Son, but the Father" (Mk. 13:32).

The fact that Jesus is the Son of God in the strict sense is implied by the unique way in which he refers to God as his Father. The term 'Father', referring to God, occurs 177 times in the Gospel. In some of these places, he is called Father in a broad sense, insofar as he is the Creator who provides for his creation (cf. Matt. 6:26), for example when Jesus counsels his hearers not to be anxious about food or clothing (cf. Matt. 6:32).

In other places, the word has a more proper sense, denoting a personal relation of men to God, for example, when Jesus speaks of alms-giving, prayer, and fasting (cf. Matt. 6:2–4, 5–6, 16–18). In these passages, the phrase used is 'your Father'. But when Jesus wishes to speak of his own relation to God, he always says: 'My Father' (cf. Matt. 7:21; Lk. 2:49). He makes a clear distinction between the way in which God is his own Father, and the way in which he is Father to his disciples: "I am ascending to my Father and your Father, to my God and your God" (Jn. 20:17). When he is speaking in his own name to God, Jesus never says 'our Father'. This phrase is found on his lips only when he is teaching his disciples how they should pray: "When *you* pray, say…" (Matt. 6:9).

When Jesus prays that his Father will take from him the chalice of the passion, it is with a unique tenderness: *Abba, Father, not as I will but as thou willest* (Mk. 14:36). His relation to almighty God is one of sonship, and of a sonship without equal. "What we saw in regard to the *logia* is true also of his prayers: *Abba*, on Jesus's lips, expresses a unique relationship with God."[8]

D. Jesus declares his unity with the Father and the Holy Spirit

Jesus of Nazareth declared that his works, performed in his Father's name, show his unity with the Father: "The Father and I are one" (Jn. 10:30). The context indicates primarily a unity of power; yet Jesus uses a deliberately general turn of phrase, to evoke the deeper mystery of his unity of *being* with the Father. And the Jews understood him in this way, attacking him for "making himself God, while being a man" (cf. Jn. 10:33).

In the final words of St Matthew's gospel, this unity is seen to embrace the Holy Spirit also, since Christ commands the apostles to baptise "in the name [singular] of the Father and of the Son and of the Holy Ghost" (Matt. 28:19): the three persons are placed on the same level. Just after this command, Jesus makes a promise which strangely echoes Isaiah's prophecy that "his name will be Emmanuel, which means *God with us*" — "And behold I am with you all days, even to the consummation of the world" (Matt. 28:20).

E. Jesus makes himself equal to God by the phrase 'Son of Man'

Jesus of Nazareth's statement of his own divinity culminated in his official testimony before the Sanhedrin. Here I refer back to what was said earlier.[9]

---

8 Joachim Jeremias, *Abba. Jésus et son Père*, Seuil, Paris, 1972, p. 69.
9 See p. 51. [page number will change once we have the page proofs]

II. THE VALUE OF JESUS'S SELF-DESCRIPTION

Can we accept what Jesus says about his messiahship, his doctrinal mission, and his divinity? When we are examining a man's testimony and we wish to know whether he is worthy to be believed, it is necessary and sufficient to determine that he is neither deceived nor a deceiver. In other words, he needs to be both competent and truthful, a person who knows of what he speaks and who is not lying.

A. Jesus's wisdom: he was not deceived

Certain rationalist scholars have tried to produce a version of events in which Jesus would have simply been mistaken in what he said of himself. Their theories do not stand up to examination. The historical method, which in this case means using the texts that we possess, cannot establish that Jesus, whose wisdom and gentleness are universally admired, was in reality a paranoiac or a fanatic or a man suffering from hallucinations. Any mere man who was convinced that he was a divine messenger, superior to all others, and who asserted that his teaching must be accepted by everyone under pain of damnation, would be an undoubted madman. All the more would someone have to be seriously unbalanced, or else blinded by a truly satanic pride, to put himself forward as equal to God and as God himself.

The character of Jesus, as made known to us in the gospels, is the very opposite of that of a fanatic. I have already mentioned the wonderful way in which Christ preached, and the extraordinary breadth of his teaching.[10] The idea that he was a proud enthusiast or a deranged dreamer is entirely incompatible with the great wisdom that appears in his teaching. It is also incompatible with his gentleness and mercy, which are apparent throughout the Gospel; with the clarity of vision which he manifests in complicated situations;[11] and with the

---

10 Cf. chapter 4.
11 Consider, for example, the episode of the woman caught in adultery (Jn. 8:7), the question about paying taxes to Caesar (Matt. 22:15–21),

CHRISTIANITY IS CREDIBLE

self-mastery which he exhibits in all circumstances, especially during his passion. Even Alfred Loisy held that both history and psychology rule out the possibility that Jesus was mad. Yet because of his rationalist prejudices, Loisy was determined not to accept that Jesus was what he claimed to be, and so he was obliged, in defiance of the demands of genuine historical criticism, to say that those parts of the Gospel where Jesus makes his highest claims are all inauthentic.[12]

Nor is it rational to seek to explain the person of Jesus by relying on an alleged affinity between genius and madness:

> When it comes to the supposed connexion between genius and madness, a question where many people have gone astray, we can say that common sense is beginning to prevail. All psychiatrists recognise that while some mad, or partially mad, persons [...] have been geniuses, their genius appeared only when, and to the extent that, they were sane.[13]

We can apply to Jesus some words of the philosopher Jean Guitton, speaking of a supposed relationship between "certain forms of instability and the highest accomplishments of the human spirit". Guitton wrote:

> Even if we supposed that some of the first disciples of Jesus had had these kinds of defect, there would still remain the problem of how people who were unwell could show more wisdom, effectiveness, prudence and courage than well-adjusted, healthy people. At each stage of Christianity's long history, we find the same phenomenon, of the weak being stronger than the strong.[14]

The simple recognition of Jesus's achievement, which is unique in history, rules out all such theories. Even the

---

and the discussion with the Sadducees about the resurrection (Matt. 22:23–32). Note also the evangelist's conclusion: "And no man was able to answer him a word; neither did any man dare from that day forth to ask him any more questions" (Matt. 22:46).

12 Cf. M. Lepin, *Le Christ Jésus*, Paris, Librairie Bloud et Gay, 1929, p. 330.
13 Léonce de Grandmaison, *Jésus-Christ. Sa personne...* p. 122–23.
14 Jean Guitton, *Jésus*, 179.

rationalist Renan had to recognise this: "A madman never succeeds. Mental aberration has never, in all history, been able to influence mankind in a lasting way."[15] In general, the opponents of orthodox Christianity, far from attributing madness to Jesus of Nazareth, have held him to be one of the wisest of the human race:

> Jesus gave religion to mankind, as Socrates gave it philosophy and as Aristotle gave it science. [...] It is Jesus who has caused mankind to take its single greatest step toward the divine. [...] Jesus is the highest of those beacons that show man whence he comes and whither he should tend. He combined in himself all that is best and highest in our nature. [...] Whatever unexpected things future ages may have in store, Jesus will not be surpassed.[16]

B. Jesus's holiness: he was not a deceiver

Already during his life-time, some of Jesus's opponents treated him as a fraud. They maintained that he was a deceiver and attributed his miracles to the devil (cf. Matt. 9:34, 12:24). Later Jewish teachers depicted him as a magician and an impostor,[17] as did a mediaeval work called *The Tale of the Three Impostors*.[18] This position is increasingly abandoned today by all those who make a serious study of the question of Jesus, including rationalist and Jewish scholars.

Recognising the groundlessness of theories that present Jesus as a deceiver, liberal and modernist critics have come up with the truly bizarre idea of a 'Jesus of faith' who has no connection with the 'Jesus of history'. As with idealistic

---

15 Ernest Renan, *Vie de Jésus*, 161.
16 Ibid., ch. 28: 'Caractères essentiels de l'œuvre de Jésus', p. 418–27.
17 We find this in the Talmud (*Sanhedrin 43a*, Babylonian Talmud) and in the *Toledoth Jeshua*, a compilation of various calumnies in circulation against Jesus.
18 This is a legend in which Jesus appears alongside Moses and Mohammed. Louis Massignon showed that it is eastern and Islamic in origin. The oldest source for it is a 9th century text, deriving from an Islamic sect called the Qarmatians. Cf. Léonce de Grandmaison, *Jésus-Christ. Sa personne...*, p. 81, note 1.

philosophy in general, where it is the mind itself which has to construct its own object, this notion is a purely arbitrary invention. Nevertheless, or perhaps for this very reason, it has found adherents, or at least partial adherents, for more than a century now, even within the Catholic Church. To me it appears to be not so much a coherent doctrine as a mental pathology, and I cannot delay over it here.

Another interesting development has been underway since the beginning of this century in Jewish studies concerning Jesus. Serious Jewish scholars tend now to abandon the old hostile arguments, and no longer mock Christianity. Reviewing one important historiographical study, Renaud Silly could write:

> Chapter IX of this book describes how Jewish studies on Jesus, since the year 2000, have reversed their whole point of view. Rather than understanding Jesus on the basis of Jewish sources, these sources themselves are now read as a response to the emergence of Christianity. This is a profound change of perspective: it means no longer looking at Jesus from a Jewish view-point, but rather trying to see how Jesus enables Jews to understand themselves. The New Testament is seen as witnessing to a state of Judaism anterior to current Jewish orthodoxy. This is the direction that has been taken by Israeli scholars, who have produced a whole crop of studies on Jesus since 2000, and their conclusions are becoming increasingly bold.[19]

C. *The character of Jesus of Nazareth*

1. HE CAN SAY PUBLICLY THAT HE IS WITHOUT SIN.

The exceptional moral character of Jesus is suggested by a fact to which there is nothing equivalent in the whole 'history of holiness': Jesus, whose humility is nonetheless plain throughout the gospel, is conscious of being 'without sin'. Faced with

---

[19] Review by Renaud Silly of Dan Jaffé, *Jésus sous la plume des historiens juifs du XXe siècle. Approche historique, perspectives historiographiques, analyses méthodologiques*, « Patrimoines : judaïsme », Paris, Cerf, 2009, in *La Revue thomiste*, 2010, pp. 404–9 [405].

a group which includes his bitterest enemies—men expert in the law, and punctilious in judging all transgressions of it, and who have been watching him closely for two and a half years—he asks: "Which of you will convict me of sin?" Would any other human being have taken such a risk? Yet his enemies are silent. By contrast, Jesus's close disciples, such as St Peter, St John, St Paul, the author of the epistle to the Hebrews, testify that it is so: "He committed no sin; in him there is no sin; he knew no sin; he experienced all our weaknesses, except sin" (1 Pet. 2:22; 1 Jn. 3:5; 2 Cor. 5:21; Heb. 4:15). Judas, who hands him over, recognises that he is just, and Pilate, who condemns him, declares that he finds in him no reason for condemnation (cf. Matt 27:4, 24).

2. HIS HOLINESS IS A TRUE MORAL MIRACLE. In all his actions, Jesus of Nazareth exhibited perfect detachment from the things of earth, and an incomparable subjection to God. His charity reveals itself by his sovereign desire for God's glory and by the fact that he fulfilled God's will even to the ultimate sacrifice. Yet unlike the false mystics, this love for God does not cause him to neglect his neighbour, nor does it lead him into the subtle pride that may be found in certain 'spiritual' people. Rather, Jesus's love for God is always accompanied with a universal charity toward all men, and with a mercy which can be surprising.

Yet Jesus also avoids false indulgence and sentimentality. He upholds the laws of divine justice, and he carries out fraternal corrections. It is striking how his lowliness and gentleness never become pusillanimity. On the contrary, they are always found united to magnanimity and to an abiding sincerity which even causes him to lose some of his disciples. Finally, his strength and his patience appear by the way in which he endures both the opposition that arises during his public life, and, above all, the torments of every kind which he suffers in his passion.

Jesus of Nazareth thus displays all the virtues, consistently, and to a heroic degree. He combines, in a supernatural way, which our minds find fascinating, moral tendencies that are naturally diverse. Thus, in him, strength and gentleness come together, as do justice and mercy, and so do the 'active' virtues of the apostolic life and the 'passive' virtues of union with God. It is not excessive to say that all this constitutes a 'moral miracle'.

This same miracle also appears from a comparison of Jesus with such founders of religions and philosophies as Mohammed[20] or Buddha[21], or even with naturally attractive figures such as Socrates[22]. We see that Jesus surpasses whatever moral perfection human beings have been able to achieve or even imagine.

3. HIS UNIQUENESS AMONG THE RELIGIOUS FIGURES OF MANKIND. The character of Jesus did not draw its inspiration from existing models, nor has it been reproduced by anyone since. It is something unequalled in human history, a fact which ought to hold the attention of anyone who is in search of religious truth. André Léonard, reflecting on "the incomparable figure of Jesus", explains that this figure is composed of three characteristics, each of which reinforces and sheds light on the other two:

> The first thing that characterises the person of Jesus is that, both in his words and his deeds, he claimed to be divine. This is wholly unique in human history. Jesus is the only man who, while being in his right mind, has claimed to be equal to God. [...] This humble claim to divinity [...] is part of the very essence of Christianity. [...]
>
> The second thing that characterises the person of Jesus stands in utter contrast to his assertion of divinity. This is the extraordinary humiliation which he undergoes

---

[20] Cf. Mark A. Gabriel, *Jésus et Mahomet. Profonds différences et suprenantes resemblances*, Romanel-sur-Lausanne, Ourania, 2009, 218 pages (reviewed in *Sedes Sapientiae*, n. 111, p. 108–10). See also the testimony of Abd-el-Jalil, quoted above, p. 64.

[21] Cf. the fine comparison of Jesus, Socrates, and Buddha, sketched by Romano Guardini, *Le Seigneur*, vol. 2, pp. 63–67; English version: *The Lord*, pp. 417–419

[22] Cf. Marie-Joseph Lagrange, *L'Évangile de Jésus-Christ, avec la synopse évangélique*, p. 655–58.

at the hour of his passion. This is a great paradox: the figure of Christ becomes disfigured. [...] [Jesus is] the only humiliated God in history. [...]

The portrait of Jesus is completed by a third thing which is, once more, unique: the testimony given to his resurrection from the dead. There is no other man in history of whom anything like this has been seriously maintained.[23]

III. IS JESUS'S SELF-DESCRIPTION THE GREATEST OF THE SIGNS?

A. Testimony as a source of knowledge

A welcome development in the recent history of thought has been the renewed awareness that *knowledge by testimony* holds a central place in human life, contrary to the claims of individualistic rationalism. Human beings are meant to live according to reason, but this is a social and not only a personal endeavour. To deny on principle that human testimony can be a source of truth is simply contrary to the facts.[24] St John Paul II noted this:

> Human beings are not made to live alone. They are born into a family and in a family they grow, eventually entering society through their activity. From birth, therefore, they are immersed in traditions which give them not only a language and a cultural formation but also a range of truths in which they believe almost instinctively. Yet personal growth and maturity imply that these same truths can be cast into doubt and evaluated through a process of critical enquiry. It may be that, after this time of transition, these truths are 'recovered' as a result of the experience of life or by dint of further reasoning. Nonetheless, there are in the life of a human being many more truths which are simply believed than truths which are acquired by way of personal verification. Who, for

---

23 André Léonard, *Les raisons de croire*, 97, 103, 104, 109.
24 Cf. Edmond Barbotin, *Le témoignage*, Brussels, Culture et vérité, « Présences, 11 », 1995; Roger Pouivet, *Qu'est-ce que croire ?*, Paris, Librairie philosophique Vrin, « Chemins philosophiques », 2003; Cyrille Michon et Roger Pouivet, *Philosophie de la religion : approches contemporaines*, Librairie philosophique Vrin, « Textes clés », 2010.

instance, could assess critically the countless scientific findings upon which modern life is based? Who could personally examine the flow of information which comes day after day from all parts of the world and which is generally accepted as true? Who, finally, could follow out all the paths of experience and thought which have yielded mankind's treasures of wisdom and religion? Man, a being who seeks the truth, is also *one who lives by belief.*[25]

Ordinary, everyday life is constantly showing us that human testimony is a reliable source of truth. While there are certainly such things as lies and deceptions, it is worth emphasising a fact often overlooked by students of epistemology: the number of false testimonies is very small in proportion to the vast number of reliable testimonies which go to make up our daily lives. This is not an accidental fact: it flows from the very nature of man, as we can see by reflecting on the two conditions for reliability, which are competence and veracity.

A witness is someone who is in a position to know the truth of what he testifies to, because he has seen it. His *competence* thus flows from the certitude which by its very nature sense-knowledge is able to afford. His *veracity*, on the other hand, has both a specific and a more general source. Its specific or proper source is man's natural love of the truth, or natural honesty: for truth is the proper object of the intelligence, our highest power, and we have a spontaneous awareness that our true human good cannot include that which is false. The more general source of veracity in human testimony is the fact that we do not act without a motive, unless we are wholly under the sway of some passion (in this case, a person acts under the influence of a cause, not for a motive, and what he does is said to be 'the act of a man' rather than 'a human act'). But the primary and general goal of man's action, for which he acts *in the absence of other considerations*, is to behave in accord with his rational nature. This explains why, in our life together in society, it is

---

25 Encyclical letter *Fides et ratio*, 31.

perfectly reasonable for us to accept each other's testimony; and experience shows that people do indeed act in this way.

It is obvious that in the human sciences, and also in the so-called 'hard sciences', knowledge is not based entirely on each person's direct experience. All research presupposes that one accepts a great number of truths that belong to other fields of study, or which have been solidly established by one's predecessors in one's own field. Without wanting to justify a naïve credulity or to deny the need for proper critical procedures, we must nevertheless recognise that while genuine "intellectual autonomy" supposes "the development of a critical faculty", it "by no means obliges us to begin by rejecting intellectual authorities, but rather, requires these".[26]

To reckon 'knowledge by testimony' as a part of human and even of scientific knowledge is simply to follow universal human practice. Yet common sense though it is, a 'scientistic' trend deriving from the 18th century Enlightenment has tended to make the domain of religion something apart from the rest of man's intellectual life. It has applied to religious matters a test of certitude which "very few of our beliefs, in any other domain, would be able to meet".[27]

B. Jesus, the "perfect witness"[28]

When we study the person of Jesus in a historical manner, as he is made known to us by the New Testament, especially by the gospels, we find that his testimony about himself is credible both negatively and positively. It is credible negatively, in the sense that his obvious wisdom and holiness, attributes which many non-Christians and agnostics also recognise in him, make it impossible that he was either a deceiver or deceived. It is credible positively, in that the moral miracle constituted by the harmony and the constancy of his virtues,

---

26 Roger Pouivet, *Qu-est ce que croire?*, p. 104.
27 Roger Pouivet, « Épistémologie de la croyance réligieuse », in Bourgeois-Gironde *et al.*, *Analyse et théologie : Croyances réligieuses et rationalité*, Librairie philosophique Vrin, 2002, p. 27–29.
28 Cf. Edmond Barbotin, *Le témoignage*, p. 79–83.

and the unique character which they reveal, even from the view-point of natural reason, are exceptional guarantees of the truth of what Jesus of Nazareth says about divine revelation: for this is the subject about which he gives testimony.

Human testimony in general is a reliable source of knowledge, provided that the criteria of competence and veracity are fulfilled. What then shall we say of the testimony of Jesus, who, as a purely historical study shows, meets these two conditions in an excellent way? Speaking to the Pharisees, Jesus himself alluded to the value of his testimony, mentioning both his competence (Jn. 8:14) and his veracity (Jn. 8:46). He said also: "The Father who sent me also bears testimony of me" (Jn. 8:18).

This 'testimony of the Father', considered as something naturally knowable, consists in divine signs and miracles, as was argued above. These constitute "an indirect proof by a sure sign"[29] of the truth of Christ's statements. But from the point of view of apologetics, one should add that the Father's testimony in favour of the Son consists above all in the *trustworthiness* of Jesus of Nazareth, which his wisdom and holiness make plain to all. This proof is still indirect, but it is *closer to the source*: that is, it is no longer the external works of the witness, but rather his own person, as it may be known from his observable conduct, which testifies in favour of what he says. Jesus leads us to his teaching via his person.

This point is both doctrinally important and spiritually consoling. If we reflect on it, recalling at the same time the testimony of the converts from Islam mentioned above, we shall be in full agreement with some words of Bernard Lucien:

> I hold (*salvo meliori judicio*, and with full submission to a possible future judgement of the magisterium) that the testimony which Christ gave to himself, *considered in the actual circumstances of his life*, is in itself a motive of credibility which is certain, and thus an objectively sufficient basis for an act of supernatural faith.[30]

---

29 Cf. chapter 3.
30 Bernard Lucien, *Apologétique. La crédibilité...*, p. 238 (italics in original).

CONCLUSION: THE KEY PLACE IN APOLOGETICS OF THE PERSON OF JESUS

The rational credibility of the message of Jesus thus depends above all on his person. This primacy, for apologetics, of the person of Jesus fits well with the passage from apologetics itself to the act of supernatural faith. There is thus in practice a continuity between apologetics and faith; this continuity derives from the divine unity of Christ, whose Person exists in two natures "without confusion or separation"[31].

> As the *Logos* made flesh (Jn. 1:14), and the human expression of the divine perfections, Jesus Christ reveals God whole and entire (Heb. 1:1). He testifies by his very being: whoever sees him sees the Father (Jn. 14:19), who is in him (Jn. 10:38); and he is the Truth (Jn. 14:6). Hence, by the very act by which he exists, Christ is at the centre and summit of all testimony; he is the 'absolute' witness. The words of Him who is the Word are simply aspects of the witness given by his very being. In him everything is a word, and a revelation of God—his works and his entire life, and especially the "good confession" of martyrdom which he gave under Pontius Pilate (1 Tim. 6:13). His word may also be called a 'confidence', since it is addressed to the human heart; to that secret, inner place where a man must make the most personal and most important decisions of his life [...].[32]

As Guérard des Lauriers said, the process preparatory to faith, by which we may form a judgement about the rational credibility of Christianity, is completed, under grace, "by a personal encounter with Christ".[33] Apologetics comes to an end by placing before us the incomparable figure of Jesus of Nazareth. This prepares the hearts of all who love the truth to encounter a supernatural mystery: Christ, the Truth incarnate.

---

31 These are two of the four words by which the Council of Chalcedon famously expressed the union of the humanity and the divinity in the incarnate Word; cf. L.-M. de Blignières, *Le mystère du Christ*, p. 58.
32 Edmond Barbotin, *Le témoignage*, p. 79.
33 M.-L. Guérard des Lauriers, *Les dimensions de la foi*, vol. 2, p. 419.

CONCLUSION

GOOD READER, THE PATH WE HAVE TAKEN has brought us, as we have just seen, to Jesus the perfect witness. We stand now on a kind of a summit. Is it the Mount of the Beatitudes where he teaches; or Mount Tabor, where his divinity appears; or Calvary, where he prays for us in his agony? All of them seem now to merge into one, as when a broad landscape is lit up all at once by the rising sun, and we look with fascination upon this unique figure, Jesus of Nazareth. We have sought the truth from our heart; we have studied his life with a genuine desire to know him. Our conscience, as we did so, seemed in silence to put to God this question: who is he?[1] We feel now that we are as if on the threshold of infinity, and that by ourselves we cannot give an answer.

Let us first of all look back from our mountain summit to the route that we have followed. Our path has gradually wound its way up the slope toward the light in which we now stand. During the first stage of our ascent, we examined the strength of the evidence concerning Jesus of Nazareth. Here, we made an important discovery: the writings of the New Testament are unique among ancient literature by the abundance of the manuscripts, their unusual closeness to the facts and the small number of significant textual variants. The process by which these writings was passed on likewise argues in favour of their genuineness and completeness, while a good number of ancient Christian witnesses offer

---

[1] In speaking of the requirements for baptism, St Peter in his first epistle mentions a disposition which the Vulgate translates as "conscientiae bonae interrogatio in Deum". Some English versions, such as the Jerusalem Bible, translate this as "a pledge made to God from a good conscience". But one can translate it more literally, and I believe more profoundly, as "the request of a good conscience made to God" (1 Pet. 3:21). The Greek word translated as *interrogatio* is *eperôtèma*, which means 'question' or 'consultation'.

corroboration of their accuracy. Various ancient historians, both Jewish and pagan, agree with the gospel accounts on certain essential points. We obtained a moral certitude of the historical character of these accounts by considering their literary genre, the personal qualities of their authors, and the weakness of the alternative hypotheses, both the 'critical' and the 'mythical'. It is reasonable to judge that Jesus of Nazareth existed and that his life was reported accurately.

We set out then on the second stage of the ascent. As we reflected on the nature of prophecy and its probative value, we encountered an undeniable fact: the Jewish expectation of a messianic saviour. This was keenly felt by the chosen people at the time of Jesus of Nazareth, so much so that it was known also to the other peoples of the East, and even among the Romans. We looked at some of the Old Testament prophecies about this Messiah and saw that Jesus of Nazareth fulfilled them. Yet not only did he fulfil certain precise prophecies; even more remarkable is that diverse aspects of the Messiah, foretold separately by the prophets, are united in him in a way which surpassed all the interpretations of the Old Testament which were current in his time. Thus, he appears at the same time as king, as suffering servant, and as a figure who is mysterious and transcendent. For those who accept the truth of the Old Testament, Jesus is the answer to the riddle which it poses; and the truth of this answer is confirmed by the fact that none of the other Jewish ideas about the Messiah has ever been realised. Yet anyone who is willing simply to make an impartial use of his reason can recognise that the monumental change which took place at that time had been prophesied in advance. The old Jewish covenant, characterised by its heavy weight of legal observances and strictly reserved to a single people, was fulfilled and at the same surpassed, by being changed into an inward and universal covenant (cf. Is. 61:1–2; Jer. 31:31–34). This "moral and religious change, brought about by Jesus's activity"[2],

---

2   Cf. M.-J. Lagrange, « Pascal et les prophéties messianiques », p. 553.

was a fact predicted in advance; no human cause can account either for the change or for the prediction. Along with men of the highest genius, such as St Thomas Aquinas and Blaise Pascal, we were greatly intrigued by this 'enduring miracle'[3], as we finished the second stage of our ascent.

Having stored away these various valuable discoveries, we pressed onwards with perseverance until we emerged onto a third level of our climb. As we scrutinised the notion of a miracle, we established first, relying simply on what natural reason can tell us about God, that miracles are possible; we then saw that their purpose must be to lead a person who is honestly seeking the truth to discover God and any revelation which he may have given; and finally we saw that when they occur in a clearly religious setting, we may distinguish with certainty between miracles on the one hand, and mere strange events or even diabolical marvels on the other. By reading the gospels, and avoiding that truncated form of human thought which is called rationalism, we saw that Jesus is said to have performed many miracles, and that the accounts of his doing so meet all the criteria of historical authenticity. We saw also how he performed them with ease, in a simple and straightforward manner. Something else struck us here: Jesus puts forward these miracles as a sure proof of his own mission, and as one of the fulfilments of ancient prophecy. At this stage of the ascent, a brightness began to appear on the horizon, and our hero was seen in the light, as it were, of a new certainty. We saw that it is credible that this man, doing what no other man has done, is what he claims to be—a messenger of God, and the Son of God.

Then we heard a voice. It was the voice of Jesus himself. It called us toward the fourth stage of the ascent, toward the light. As we went on, keeping hold of the rope which joined us to the lower levels, we paid close attention to this voice. And like the apostles on the roads of Galilee, or like the disciples who were with him on the Mount of the

---

3 Blaise Pascal, *Pensées*, n. 706.

Beatitudes or the shores of the lake, or even like the Jews who used with sincerity to listen to him in the Temple, we were won over. With the temple guard, we said: "No man ever spoke like this man" (Jn. 7:46). He has a message to communicate, and he does so with simplicity and authority, at once touching men's hearts and enlightening their minds. He talks to the people of one particular time, speaking with his deep voice in the beautiful Aramaic language. He teaches a fascinating combination of truths: natural truths about God and man; supernatural mysteries that were hidden for ages in the silence of God; truths about our actions, and how they must follow a law of love that leads to the beatitudes. It all formed a sublime harmony, uniquely satisfying to the mind and acting powerfully upon the will. Nor were our senses neglected, or our imagination: for they were captivated by the poetry of his words and the poetry, also, of his merciful deeds. The divine origin of his teaching was already well established, as on a rock, by the prophecies he fulfilled and the miracles he wrought. But it was confirmed for us, and beautifully, by the perfection of what he said and the nobility of what he did.

But we have not yet finished the climb. To reach the top, we must cross over a precipice: the shameful passion and death of Jesus of Nazareth. And so, along with the apostles and the disciples who were witnesses to those events, we formed a chain to help us reach the fifth stage. Can we pass through the hour of the Power of darkness, and come once more to the light? Let us hear what the witnesses say. They tell us that Jesus foresaw his resurrection, that they themselves know that he died, that they saw and touched him after he had risen again. The context shows that there was here neither deceit nor hallucination. The evidence accumulates for forty days: the empty tomb, the testimony of the soldiers, that of the women, the apostles, and the disciples, the dramatic change in their behaviour, and their firmness even to martyrdom in bearing witness that Jesus has risen again.

CHRISTIANITY IS CREDIBLE

The resurrection is like a peak which crowns our intellectual mountaineering. From here we can look back and see the sure path which has brought us this far: prophecies, miracles, and teaching. From this height, the route we have taken appears more distinctly; and as we look at it, our certainty grows, and we come to see the resurrection of Jesus of Nazareth as a complete proof of Christianity. We feel, too, how this religion is different from all other religions and philosophies. Only Christianity offers us a salvation able to give a meaning to suffering, and which triumphs over absurdity and death: in short, a salvation that is complete.

Can we go any higher? Can we achieve a still deeper conviction of its credibility, like a mountaineer fixing his pickaxe even deeper in the ground? Indeed we can: there is a sixth and final stage, to which we must ascend, as it were, by a sheer rock-face. Yet, paradoxically, this is also the securest part of our climb. Here we listen to the words of Jesus as he speaks about himself. It is plain that he is not mad nor evil; neither deceived nor a deceiver. His personality is unique, beyond that of all other religious figures in the history of mankind. He is a reliable witness; and he himself has said who he is—the Son of God, seated at the right of the Power. It is entirely rational to accept his testimony about himself, and to grant that he is exactly who he claims to be. Christianity is indeed credible.

But here, good reader, apologetics comes to an end. It has done its work by creating conditions that can enable you to believe more readily, and from the heart. But if your path is to bring you out into the Day, into the very mystery of Christ, this can happen only by means of a mysterious marriage: the marriage of free will and of grace. *The path of the just, as a shining light, goeth forwards and increaseth even to perfect day* (Prov. 4:18).

APPENDIX

The Appearances of the Risen Christ

THE LIKELY SEQUENCE OF EVENTS ACCORDing to M.-J. Lagrange OP[1]

The resurrection at the end of the night (dawn beginning to appear), appearance to the Blessed Virgin (?)	The women leave to go to the tomb
An earthquake, the descent of the angel, the stone rolled away, the soldiers "terrified and like dead men". The soldiers flee and tell the chief-priests what has happened.	
Mary Magdalene arrives at the tomb by herself and sees that the stone has been rolled away. She runs to tell Peter and John.	The other women buy spices. They enter the tomb, see that it is empty, see an angel or angels, and are told about the resurrection. They keep silent.
Peter and John run to the tomb, enter, see the linen cloths on the ground and the sudarium which had been around his head, not with the linen cloths but rolled up by itself in its place. John's faith is awakened by seeing this: "He saw and believed" (Jn. 20:9).[2]	
Mary Magdalen returns to the tomb and sees the Lord (1st 'Christophany')	The women speak to the apostles and the disciples, who don't believe them. Two disciples set off for Emmaus.

---

[1] Cf. C. Lavergne, *Synopse des quatre Évangiles en français, d'après la synopse grecque du R. P. M.-J. Lagrange, o.p.*, Paris, Librairie Lecoffre, J. Gabalda et Cie, 1974, nn. 306–20, pp. 254–63.

[2] Cf. Vittorio Messori, Ils disent: « Il est ressucité » ; see p. 144, n. 15.

Mary Magdalene tells the disciples that she has seen the Lord, but they do not believe her.

Jesus is seen (*ôpthè*) by Simon Peter in the afternoon of Easter Sunday (2nd Christophany, mentioned as a fact by Luke and Paul, but without any details being given).

At the end of the afternoon, Jesus causes himself to be recognised by the two disciples on the way to Emmaus (3rd Christophany); these return that evening to the Eleven and to the others, "who do not believe them either" (Mk. 16:13).

While all apart from Thomas are present, Jesus "stood in the middle of them", and rebukes their unbelief. They touch him, and Jesus eats in their presence (4th Christophany).

Eight days later, Jesus appears to the disciples, including Thomas, who touches his wounds (5th Christophany).

Appearance on the shore of Lake Tiberias; the miraculous draught of fish; the bestowal of the primacy upon Peter (6th Christophany).

Appearance on a mountain in Galilee; the great commission (7th Christophany).

Appearance to more than 500 brethren (8th Christophany)

Appearance to James (9th Christophany)

Last Christophany, before the Ascension, in Jerusalem.

ABOUT THE AUTHOR

FR LOUIS-MARIE DE BLIGNIÈRES was born in Madrid in 1949, to French parents who were also practising Catholics. His father was at that time an army officer on active duty, and his mother was living with her own father, an engineer in a Spanish mining company. After a traditional secondary education in Paris, Fr Louis-Marie pursued scientific studies at university, and gained a master's degree in Astrophysics in 1972. He passed through a period of atheism, during which time he nevertheless continued to admire Catholicism and Christian civilisation. He returned to the practice of the faith in 1970, during an Ignatian retreat preached at a Benedictine abbey dedicated to the Blessed Virgin Mary. His time as an agnostic and his subsequent conversion has left him with a keen desire to explain and defend the rational credibility of the Christian faith.

In 1972, he discovered again the vocation that he had first sensed as a child. After studies at a Benedictine monastery, and then at the seminary of Ecône in Switzerland, he was ordained priest in 1977 by Archbishop Lefebvre, as an oblate of what would become the abbey of Barroux in France. In 1979, he founded the Fraternity of St Vincent Ferrer in western France, between Le Mans and Rennes. This institute is Dominican in its spirituality, though distinct from the Order of Preachers. It is characterized by a traditional religious observance, the place of St Thomas Aquinas in its life of study, the use of the Dominican liturgical books in force in 1962, and a doctrinal preaching that takes many forms, especially that of retreats on the mysteries of the rosary.

In 1988, after the publication of the 'motu proprio' *Ecclesia Dei*, the Fraternity became a religious institute of pontifical right. It currently has 21 members, of whom 14 are priests, including several with canonical doctorates in theology, canon law and philosophy.

Fr Louis-Marie obtained a doctorate in metaphysics in 2003, at the university of Paris-Sorbonne. He has written several books of theology and spirituality, and he is the author of many articles in *Sedes Sapientiae*, the Fraternity's journal. In 2022, a special edition of this journal was published in English.

www.ingramcontent.com/pod-product-compliance
Lightning Source LLC
Chambersburg PA
CBHW020242010526
44107CB00038B/1448/J